MONEY SKILLS AND PERSONAL FINANCE FOR TEENS MADE EASY

YOUR STEP-BY-STEP GUIDE TO BUDGETING, SAVING, AND INVESTING THAT WILL DEVELOP SMART MONEY HABITS AND UNLOCK FINANCIAL FREEDOM FOR LIFE

RILEY WEALTH

TABLE OF CONTENTS

INTRODUCTION

Okay, you're scrolling through TikTok, and you see that awesome game setup you really crave. Or maybe those concert tickets are finally out! Or perhaps that laptop you need for college. It doesn't really matter what you set your eyes on; all you know is that your heart does that little excited jump. But then reality hits. You see the price, and you're pretty sure the price tag is laughing at your empty wallet. You double-check—it isn't; price tags don't laugh, but for a second there, it really did seem like it. Anyway, the truth is, we've all been there—wanting something so badly, just to have our dreams of obtaining it come crashing down when we look at its price. But what if the price tag doesn't have to be a dream-crusher? What if there was a way for you to make your money (yes, regardless of how much you have right now) work for you? And by the way, anything counts: birthday money, allowance, your weekend job; money is money. It doesn't matter where it comes from.

But let's first get to the main question: Why am I here? Well, I was you not that long ago. I was that kid who burned through money fast. Like *really* fast. Faster than my phone battery would go into "saving mode" (doesn't it feel like it's always in saving mode?). You see, no one taught me how money works. I could do the math, sure. I am not a genius, but I could get by in math class. But nobody showed me how to make smart choices with my actual money, and that's why I'm here. That's why I developed this passion for financial education so you don't have to go through this—through a lack of financial literacy like I did. This is what drove me to write my first book, *Investing for Teenagers Made Simple: Your Step-by-Step Path to Obtaining Wealth and Financial Freedom Quickly*. By the way, the response was overwhelming; thank you very much, and it turns out I wasn't the only one who needed this stuff!

But this book is different, not only from my first book that focuses on investments but from other personal finance books for teenagers. Is it not some long, boring book with complex terms that makes you fall asleep like it's a history class or something. This is a guide—your personal money guide—written specifically for you and your world—the world of Apple Pay, Venmo, and everything else teens use today.

Now, what will you find inside? Without boring you with details, the book is designed to tackle real-life situations right now:

- Want to know if you can start investing with only $20? We'll cover that.
- Thinking about getting a debit or credit card but don't know how to convince your parents? I got you.
- Need to find out how to save for college without giving up your social life? We'll work on that too.

Now you'll also find:

- real stories from teens who've completely crushed their goals.
- interactive challenges you can actually use (and enjoy!).
- digital tools and apps that make managing money way easier.
- clear and concise explanations without that boring financial jargon.

You might still be wondering why all of this matters. Well, 83% of teens who learn about money management early end up way better at handling their finances as they grow up (Bai, 2023). What does this mean? The things you learn could be the difference between struggling with money and having the freedom to live the life of your dreams on your own terms.

As Warren Buffett puts it (you might not know about him yet, but you will): *The best investment you can make is in yourself.* And this is exactly what we're doing here.

So, grab your notebook (or your Notes app, since hardly anyone uses paper these days), and as you read through this book, jot down ideas, questions, and your money goals because you will start planning your financial freedom journey.

Now, before we get to it, let me just say that I get it. I really do. Money talk can be overwhelming, dull, or just plain confusing. But I'm aware of this, you see, and I can guarantee you that you will not feel this way as you read this book. And by the end of it, you will look at money differently. You will have the knowledge and confidence to make smarter choices with the cash you have, start building wealth (yes, right now), and set yourself up for a fantastic financial future. So, let's get to it!

1

UNDERSTANDING MONEY BASICS

Have you ever bought something on Amazon and thought, *Hold on... where does that money go?* Or has your friend ever sent you $10 through Venmo for pizza night, and you wondered, *How does this even work?* Well, plenty of people ask those same questions. Most of us don't really understand how money works behind the scenes—it just does, right? Until it doesn't, of course.

Say you just got $100 for your birthday (thank you, Grandma!). That bill in your hand—or balance in your Cash App—is more interesting than it seems. Our money system has come a long way since ancient times. People once traded seashells for food, and now we tap smartphones to buy smoothies after school. The foundation hasn't changed, but it's evolved in ways that would leave our ancestors speechless.

So, what exactly are we going to talk about in this chapter? As you might have guessed, one of the main topics is decoding the mysteries of money, such as:

- Why does the $20 bill in my pocket have value?
- How does my money travel through the economy?
- What do banks actually do with my money?
- Why do I care about taxes?
- How do I create a budget that doesn't make me want to scream?

These are the basics, and once you understand them, everything will start falling into place. So, let's get to it.

WHAT IS MONEY REALLY ABOUT? UNDERSTANDING CURRENCY AND VALUE

Okay, one thing I want to highlight here is that money isn't just the cash you have in your pocket or that number on your online banking app. Money is more about value and trust. Sounds a little weird, I know. How can money be about trust? Well, think of a video game such as Fortnite or Roblox. They have their own currency, right? Fortnite uses V-bucks, and Roblox uses Robux.

That money is not "real" in the sense that you can't spend it at the grocery store, but people spend real dollars to get it. Why? Well, they trust those currencies hold value in the game world—and that value and trust are what matters.

Remember that example I gave about the people in ancient times who used seashells as currency? Well, throughout history, people used the weirdest stuff as money. Pacific Islanders, for example, used giant stone wheels, which were too heavy to move, so ownership was passed by word of mouth. Ancient Romans used salt, which is where the phrase "worth their weight in salt" comes from (EricT_CulinaryLore, 2012). Some cultures even used cattle. Just imagine going around the market with three cows to buy some eggs—wouldn't that be a sight to see?

When Does Money Become Money?

So, the question here is: When does money become money? Well, in theory, for something to work as money, there are three prerequisites:

Medium of Exchange

This means the money needs to work everywhere. Instead of trading an egg for a bag of color, you use a currency that is universally accepted. Imagine going to the market with three eggs to get a jug of milk. What if the milkman doesn't need eggs that day and wants to be paid in bread instead? Without a common medium of exchange, bartering becomes complicated and inefficient. Money solves this by acting as a go-between that everyone agrees on—like the universal "yes" of transactions. Then, you'd be able to go home with your jar of milk instead of leaving empty-handed.

Unit of Account

Think of this as the price tag. Money helps us measure the value of things, making it easier to compare prices. It gives you perspective —are those $150 sneakers really worth two full days of work at your part-time job? Or consider this: When you're saving up for something, money makes it easier to track how close you are to your goal. It turns value into a number we all understand.

Store of Value

As the name "store of value" suggests, you can save today's work for tomorrow's spending. For example, eggs are a terrible currency. They just spoil in a few weeks. But money doesn't get stale, go rotten, or expire. You can store it safely and use it whenever you're ready.

The Trust: Why We Believe in Money?

To put it simply: because everybody else does. Money has no real value outside a human's brain. Give a monkey the choice of a $50 bill and a banana. I guarantee you that the monkey will pick the banana every time—even though that $50 could buy it more than one banana. The cash in your pocket is just a piece of paper that we, as humans, believe is worth something. It's like a collective lie.

This is also why Pokémon cards can sometimes be worth hundreds or even thousands of dollars. It's just cardboard and ink, but collectors unanimously agree that they're valuable. The same goes for Bitcoin, gold, and other precious metals.

Money Around the World

Lately, money has been transforming and is becoming more digital. To give you an example: In Sweden, almost no one uses cash anymore—everything's digital. Meanwhile, in Japan, people still like to carry cash. Some countries use multiple currencies in daily life (I know, confusing!). In the US, your dollars might buy you more or less in different countries. Sometimes, those really nice sneakers are way cheaper abroad.

In today's world, it hardly matters where you live—you can send and receive money in seconds or buy something from anywhere while sitting in your bedroom. It's all super interconnected. So, just to wrap this section up: Money is trust and value, and above all, it makes life easier. Once you get this, you will start seeing money differently, and you can make it work for you.

THE JOURNEY OF A DOLLAR: HOW MONEY MOVES IN THE ECONOMY

We are all on a journey, and so is money. Have you ever wondered where that bill in your pocket has been before it reached your hands or where your money goes after you tap your phone to pay for your pumpkin latte at Starbucks? Well, this is exactly what we will be looking at in this section. Let's track that $20 bill you have in your wallet. It all starts in the Federal Reserve (the money's birthplace). First, your bill heads to a local bank, then maybe your parents withdraw it to give you an allowance (it might have crossed the country before that; we don't know, but let's assume it's brand new). Then, you spend that $20 at your local cafe while hanging out with your friends. Now, the cafe owner has it and uses it to pay their employee's wages (also, let's assume he pays cash). That employee uses that $20 to pay for groceries. The grocery store uses it to pay their supplier, and the supplier pays their truck driver… and it goes on and on. It might even end up in your pocket again (but probably not). What does this mean? Well, this means that your $20 bill has helped many people get what they need. Impressive, right?

Making Waves in the Economy

The cool bit here is that when you spend money, you're actually part of something much, much bigger. Say that you and your friends all saved up to buy new gaming consoles. When a lot of different people do this, here's what happens:

- The gaming store makes money.
- They are able to hire more workers.
- Those workers now have money to spend.
- Maybe they will go to your parent's restaurant.
- Your parent's business does better.
- And maybe (just maybe) you get a bigger allowance.

Of course, more often than not, the consequences of our spending don't affect us directly, but they do impact and benefit others.

The Money Multiplier

Now, let's get to something really interesting. What do you think happens when you put your money in the bank? If you don't know any better, you might think they lock it in a vault or assign it to your banking app. But no! The bank actually lends out most of your money to other people while still letting you access your full balance whenever you want. But how? Well, when multiple people deposit their money into the same bank, it just kind of works—assuming not every customer withdraws their money all at once. Let me give you a real-world example:

You deposit $100 from your birthday money (thank you, Grandma!). The bank keeps some of it (let's say they keep $10) but lends $90 to someone who wants to start a small business selling custom sneakers. That business owner uses the $90 to buy supplies and pays the supplier, who then deposits that money into their bank account. You probably know where this is going, right? The cycle begins all over again. Your original $100 didn't just help you; it helped the bank, the business owner, their supplier, and everyone else down the line. This is what economists call the "multiplier effect."

BANKS AND YOU: HOW THEY WORK AND WHY THEY MATTER

I think the best way to understand banks is to think of them as an advanced piggy bank, but they do far more than just hold your money.

What Banks Really Do

I know movies give us the impression that banks are just vaults and security guards, but the reality is not quite like that. When you start earning money, even through an allowance or your first part-time job, you will want to have somewhere to deposit that money. As we've seen, your money doesn't just stay there; it goes around helping other people. But there's a fascinating thing I've yet to mention: interest. Banks can actually pay you to keep your money with them, and as you might have guessed, that's called interest. Let me give you a simple example. You save $1,000 for college. The bank might pay you 2% interest per year without you doing anything other than keep your money there. If you do this, by the end of the year, you will have $1,020. It doesn't look like much, but the more you deposit and the longer you leave it there, the more it will grow.

Okay, but not everything is perfect. If the bank lends you money, they charge you interest, too, and it is often higher than the interest you receive. So, if you get a $1,000 loan at 5% interest, at the end of the year, you will have to repay $1,050. That's actually how banks make money. However, loans are not necessarily bad if you need the money and can pay it back, but we will get to this later.

Keeping Your Money Safe

There might be a question lingering on your mind: "Can banks lose my money?" Well, this is very unlikely, and if, for some reason, they do, you're usually covered. There's this organization called the Federal Deposit Insurance Corporation (FDIC), and they basically insure your money (usually up to $250,000) (FDIC, 2024). Also, in the UK, this organization is called the Financial Services

Compensation Scheme (FDCS) and protects individuals to up to £85,000 (FSCS, n.d.). In Canada, the equivalent organization is called the Canada Deposit Insurance Corporation (CDIC) and has a protection limit of CAD $100,000 (*What Is the CDIC?*, n.d.). So, while it is very (and I mean *very*) unlikely your bank somehow loses your money, you are still insured. Besides that, your money is also protected by very strict government rules that banks have to follow, high-tech security systems, multiple backups of all your information, and regular checks to make sure banks are playing by the rules.

Modern Banking Services

You might be aware of many of the things I'm going to talk about here. But nowadays, banking is very different from what it was just a few years ago. You no longer have to go to the bank building to manage your money (I know people who haven't set foot in an actual bank in years). Today's banking management is at the tip of your fingers, right on your phone or computer.

Straight from there, you can check your balance, send money to friends, set up automatic savings, get alerts if there's some suspicious activity on your account, deposit checks just by taking a picture, and track your spending to see how far you are from your goals. But the best part is that most banks offer special accounts for teens, giving you zero monthly fees, no minimum balance requirements, and a lot more that we will talk about later.

MAKING SENSE OF TAXES: BASICS EVERY TEEN SHOULD KNOW

Hardly anyone gets excited about taxes. But before you lose interest and skip this section entirely, just hear me out for a second. Taxes won't go anywhere, so you might as well understand them. And truth be told, they are not that complicated.

Why Do We Even Pay Taxes?

You know that park you love to spend time in with your friends? Taxes paid for that. That new chemistry lab at your school where your teacher shows you all those crazy experiments? Taxes paid for that too. To put it simply, taxes are when everyone chips in to get nice stuff that everyone can enjoy. Your taxes to make your town, state, and country run. They pay for roads, schools' football fields, public libraries (yes, with the free Wi-Fi), local pools, and even street lights at night.

Different Flavors of Taxes

Now, there are many different types of taxes. Let's get to them.

- Sales Tax: This is likely the first tax you notice when you see a video game with a price tag of $60 and at checkout costs $65. That's sales taxes. Now, each state in the US has its own rate, which is why the same game might have a different cost in different states.
- Income Tax: If you're already working, even as a part-timer, you are probably familiar with income tax. This is money taken from your paycheck before you get it. You might notice a discrepancy in your pay stub between gross and net payments, and that's the taxes taken from you. But we will get to this later on.
- Property tax: While you probably don't pay this yet, your parents probably do. This money often goes to your local government to pay for schools, parks, etc.

Your First Job, Your First Taxes

If you have a part-time job, there's probably something your boss has omitted: If you're making more than $12,950 (as of 2024) a year, chances are you will have to file a tax return (IRS, n.d.). Don't start panicking; it's fairly simple. It goes something like this:

At the start of your job, you will fill out a form called a W-4, which essentially tells the government that this is you and you're working now. Throughout the year, money gets taken from your paychecks automatically, which are called withholdings. Early next year, your employer will give you the W-2 form showing how much you made and how much tax you've already paid. Then, you (or, more likely, your parents, at first) file a tax return. There's the chance that you might get money back if you overpaid taxes (but don't hold your breath).

Pro Tips for Teen Taxpayers

If you're starting your first job, there are a few things you can do to make it easier when it comes to your taxes:

- Keep track of all your documents. I recommend creating a folder (digital or physical) for anything that says "Important Tax Document."
- Don't ignore tax forms when they come in the mail or email. Chances are that they are important.
- Ask your parents about being claimed as a dependent since it affects how you file your taxes.
- If you're making money from a side hustle (such as selling things online or doing any type of creative work), you might need to track that income too.

So, taxes might be a little annoying, but I'm not saying they are. They take some of your money, but they allow you to participate in society. Understanding them now, while the stakes are definitely lower, will make you way more confident later on in life when they will cost more.

ALL ABOUT BUDGETING: WHY AND HOW TO START

Here's another topic that, at first glance, might sound a little boring: budget. But it's not. Not in the slightest. A budget is a way to get things you want. It's pretty much like creating a game plan for your money—like strategizing to beat a tough boss in a video game.

Why Budgeting Actually Matters

So, it's a Friday night, and you're hanging out with your friends. It's time to order some food, but you spent your last $20 on that new video game earlier. Awkward... See, if you had a budget, this situation wouldn't happen to you. However, keep in mind that budgeting is not about restricting yourself. In fact, it's about freedom. It's knowing that you can say "yes" to a concert ticket because you've planned for it. It's never having to ask your parents for extra money because you've got everything (at least money-wise) figured out.

Creating Your First Budget Without Losing Your Mind

I want to make this super simple. Essentially, you have to organize things in a way that makes sense to you. So, here's how you can start:

- First, figure out your income. This could be a part-time job, allowance, birthday money, side hustles, or anything else.
- Track your spending for a week.
- Write down your regular expenses.
- List your saving goals.

With that done, you then have to create the actual plan.

- Split your money into three main categories:
  - must-haves (phone bill, bus fare, lunch money)
  - want-to-haves (movies, video games, snacks, outings with friends)
  - future-you fund (savings for bigger goals, e.g., paying for college tuition)

Pretty simple, right? But it gets simpler.

Tech to the Rescue

Before your time, people had to open Excel and create a complicated spreadsheet to make their budgets. While you can still do that, apps can make this super easy. There are some great apps out there that can track your spending automatically, send you alerts before you overspend, help you get back on track with your savings, and even link to your bank account so you can have everything in real-time.

To give you a few examples, you have:

- Squirrel
- Wally
- Splitwise
- Chip

There are many others, and you can research for yourself, but these are a great place to start.

Let me also give you some tips on budgeting depending on your circumstances. If your only income source is allowances, it's best to break your allowance into weekly amounts. Then, set aside a portion for savings before you start spending. Also, keep a small emergency fund in case there's a situation where you might need to use it.

If you have a part-time job, the first thing I would recommend is to set aside tax money (trust me when I tell you, your future self will be grateful). Then, you can automate your savings, which means your bank account will automatically send a portion of your income to a savings account. This makes it a lot easier for you to save. But don't forget to give yourself a "fun money" limit each week so you don't overspend.

For those with side hustles and an irregular income, you have to keep track of this income. I would say save a bigger percentage since you don't know when the next payment will come. Create a separate fund for business expenses, as you might be able to lower your taxes with it.

2

SMART BUDGETING AND SAVING

I 'm sure you know the feeling when you want something but just don't have enough money saved to get it. Maybe it's concert tickets or the latest iPhone—whatever it is, we've all been there. However, there are ways to make sure this doesn't happen, or at least doesn't happen that often, as I've hinted at before. In this chapter, you'll learn to level up your money skills, much like a character in a video game levels up by getting all the best gear available. Of course, in this case, it is about your real-life finances.

You will learn all about creating a budget that actually works for you and your lifestyle, as well as how to make your savings grow like magic through compound interest. So, here's a quick break-down of the main topics.

The first thing we will get to is how to design your personalized budget—one that works for you regardless of the type of income you have. Then, we will look into the art of saving money without feeling like you're missing out on life by setting practical goals that make sense. Finally, we explore compound interest—how people get to make money while they sleep.

Besides that, we'll also crack the code of smart shopping because, whether we like it or not, we all spend money—so we might as well spend it wisely. The last topic we'll cover is emergency funds: your financial safety net for when life decides to be unexpected.

DESIGN YOUR FIRST BUDGET

If I had to compare budgeting to something more fun, I would pick designing a character. There are many similarities to it, as you will see. When creating a character in a role-playing game (RPG), you have to pick their skills and gear, right? Well, with budgeting, you are setting up a great system to level up your money game.

Understanding Your Money Flow

Before we get into the tools and tricks, let's talk about your relationship with money. At your age, your income probably comes from different sources: allowances, part-time jobs, or even online businesses you might have set up. You might also have different expenses—daily stuff like lunch money or bus fares, as well as saving up for your goals. So, knowing where your money comes from and where it goes is the map you need to understand your financial world.

Picking Your Perfect Budget Tool

Now, with budgeting apps on your smartphone, like EveryDollar, it's like having a personal financial assistant track every dollar, send you reminders, and create graphs for you to better understand where your money is going. If you don't want to use apps, you can go old-school and use a spreadsheet like Excel or Google Docs and track your spending that way.

Setting Goals That Actually Work

This is the part where you set up goals that get you pumped about savings. The first thing you have to do is to be specific. Don't just say you are *going* to save; make sure you know *what* you are saving for and make a plan. If you want to buy the new iPhone in the next four months, understand how much you have to save every month to reach that goal.

Your goals are like missions in video games: The short-term goals are the daily quests, the medium-term goals are weekly challenges, and the long-term goals are the epic quests.

Most importantly, these goals have to be realistic. If you're making $500 a month at your part-time job, you likely won't be able to save $1,000 in a month (unless you have multiple sources of income). But saving $100? That is possible.

Regular Check-Ins

Your budget should grow with you. You don't use the same strategy every single level in a video game, right? Sometimes, a level requires you to change things up. It is the same for your budget—you need regular updates and check-ins to match your budget with changes in your life. Set aside some time each week to check your progress and any necessary changes to your goals and strategy.

SAVING SMARTS: SETTING AND ACHIEVING YOUR FINANCIAL GOALS

Let's now talk about turning those dreams into reality, regardless of what those dreams are. Whether it's owning a car, traveling the world, or buying a new laptop, saving is the first step. While it might not seem like the most exciting thing in the world (mainly because you're just starting), saving can actually be pretty fun.

Goal-Oriented Saving: Making Your Dreams Real

When you really want something but don't know how to get it, you should turn to SMART goals. Essentially, this means setting your goals to be *specific*, m*easurable*, a*chievable*, r*elevant*, and t*ime-bound*. The best way to explain how this works is through a story. James was desperate to get his hands on a PS5 (who isn't?). Rather than just dreaming about it, he got smart about it (yes, pun intended here). He figured out the exact cost: $500, which was enough for the console and that one game he wanted to play really badly. After doing some quick math, he realized he could sock away $50 a month for it. Yes, 10 months seemed like forever, but with his plan, it was doable. Every month, he could see he was getting closer to his goal.

How is this a SMART goal? Well, let's look at the definition:

Was James' goal specific? Quite, right? He wanted a PS5 and a game. Was it measurable? Sure, he knew how much he needed and how much he needed to save each month to get it. Was it achievable? Yes, it took 10 months, but he achieved it. Was it relevant? For James, yes. And time-bound? Yes, 10 months.

Juggling Multiple Savings Goals

In life, we often don't just save for one thing. You could be saving for a PS5, a trip with your friends next summer, and your first car in a couple of years—all at the same time. It can feel a little overwhelming to balance multiple goals, but the good news is you don't have to pick just one. Just like you don't give 100% of your time to just one activity—whether it's school, hobbies, or hanging out with your friends—you don't have to dedicate every single saved dollar toward just one goal.

Keeping Motivation Going

This ties up with juggling multiple savings goals. You will have short-, medium-, and long-term goals, and when you accomplish the short- or medium-term goals, you will be more motivated to reach the long-term ones. There will be times when waiting for your goal will feel like you're stuck on the loading page at 99% for what seems like hours. It will be tempting to just give up and spend your money on other things. Obviously, you shouldn't, and there's a little trick to it: the "set it and forget it" method. You can set automatic transfers from your allowance or part-time job income into your savings (you can talk to your parents about this if they are the ones responsible for your bank account). The second the money hits your account, part of it will go straight to your savings without a chance for you to see it.

Making It Visual

For most of us, numbers are boring. If this is not the case for you… hmm, just keep going, I guess? However, many of us are more visual. And visual tools make it a great way to check on your progress. Just like a progress bar on a video game, but in this case, it shows how close you are to your goal.

Let me tell you a story about a girl named Monica. She wanted to save up for this massive gaming convention next summer. You know how we often get carried away by other things in life and forget our goals? Well, to make sure she didn't, the very first thing she did was change her phone's wallpaper into a visual tracker. Every single time she opened her phone (which was quite a lot), she saw how close she was to her goal.

THE POWER OF COMPOUND INTEREST IN SAVING

Of all the techniques, strategies, and tricks I'm going to talk about in this section, compound interest is perhaps the most significant because of how much it can change your savings. It's like a cheat code but totally legal and, well, honest. To better explain how this works, let's get into another story before developing the concept.

Compound Interest Explained

Two good friends—Jordan and Taylor—got $1000 from their grandparents after they graduated. Taylor was super excited and immediately bought the latest iPhone. Jordan did something different and put his money in a high-yield savings account, paying 4% interest annually. It sounds quite boring, right? Taylor thought that, too, but we're not there yet. After a year, Jordan's money grew to $1,040. Well, it's not a life-changing sum by any means, but over the following year, the interest started to earn interest too.

The Long Game: Watch Your Money Grow

After five years, Jordan's account grew to over $1,216 without adding a single dollar to it. Meanwhile, Taylor's iPhone was completely outdated. But here's where it gets even better. Let's fast forward to, say, 10 years. Think about saving for college or that car you really want. If you start putting just $50 aside every month from your income with compound interest, you are not just saving $600—you're earning much more.

Starting Early: Your Future Self Will Thank You

As I've mentioned, starting earlier will give you a massive head start in this race to become financially free. If you start saving $100 a month at the age of 15 in an account earning 5% interest, by the time you are 25, you will have more than $12,000 from your contributions alone. Thanks to compound interest, you'd have over $15,000, which means you'd earn $3,500 for free!

Making Your Money Work Harder: Reinvestment Strategies

Here's a tip (honestly, write it down): When your savings account pays you interest, you can set it in a way so that the interest automatically goes back into your account to earn even more interest. This is called reinvesting. Most banks allow you to do this automatically, so you don't have to manually do it every time you earn interest.

This is the way to make your money work even harder than you. You could be sleeping, hanging out with your friends, or studying —your money is working.

SMART SHOPPING: HOW TO SAVE MONEY ON EVERYDAY PURCHASES

There are very few things that can beat buying something new (even if this ecstatic feeling only lasts a couple of minutes or hours). I'm not denying that there is fun in spending money, but there are ways you can do it without completely destroying your budget, savings, or wallet.

You might remember when you impulsively bought that t-shirt that said "Only $25"—why not, right? But then, a few days later, you found the exact same t-shirt for $15. It happens to many of us.

That's why I'm going to share some tricks with you when it comes to shopping.

The Art of the Deal

I had a friend, Zack, who thought coupons were something the old generation did until he found out he could get his Starbucks coffee for half the price through their rewards app. This doesn't end here. I'm sure your favorite brands already have loyalty or student programs that offer discounts. Another thing you should pay attention to is sales patterns since most stores have a predictable cycle. When you want new clothes, the end of the season is the best time to get them. If you're into gaming, Steam has major sales in the winter and summer. Black Friday is another great day to get more tech stuff for a discounted price.

Buy Nice or Buy Twice

Oftentimes, spending more is actually cheaper. I learned this the hard way. Over the course of a school year, I bought three cheap backpacks for a total of $100. The following year, I bought one good backpack for $90 that lasted for years to come. In fact, I still have it somewhere, and it is still nearly in perfect condition.

Think of it this way. If you buy $20 earbuds every two months because they keep breaking, that's $120 a year. You could buy one good pair for $80 that could actually last more than a year. Even if they only last a year, you've already saved $40.

Your Phone: Your Secret Shopping Weapon

Your phone can be the best tool you have when it comes to shopping. Let's talk about some apps and programs that can come in handy. Say you want a hoodie. If you use the Honey browser extension, you can track the hoodie you want, and once it goes on sale, you'll get a notification. ShopSavvy is another cool app that lets you scan barcodes to compare prices across different stores.

Let me give you a quick tip. Make a list of things you want but don't need urgently. Then, keep track of the prices of these items for a few weeks before buying. This way, you will find the best deals, and it gives you the time to really consider if you want that thing.

EMERGENCY FUNDS: WHY AND HOW MUCH?

Let me give you a scenario of a real emergency: Your phone suddenly dies just before an important group project is due. Doesn't it seem that disasters always happen at the worst possible time? If you have an emergency fund, you can be safer or at least have something to fall back on. Here's a relevant story that did happen to someone I know. Let's call this person Maya.

Maya rode her bike to her part-time job, but it got stolen. Without an emergency fund, she would have been stuck either walking three miles each way (not ideal) or asking her parents for rides. Thankfully, she had been smart and tucked away some money each month. Not a day had passed, and she already had a new (used) bike.

How Much Do You Really Need?

You might be thinking: *Why would a teenager need an emergency fund?* It worked wonders for Maya. She was independent enough to solve the issue by herself without asking her parents for money. Isn't that what many teens want? More independence? Facing their own problems? Anyway, to answer the question in the heading:

There's not one right answer, but there's a realistic way to think of this, of course.

While not the happiest thought in the world, you can start thinking about what could go wrong. Here are a few examples:

- a phone repair (could be anywhere from $50 and $200)
- a new laptop for school ($400+)
- emergency Uber rides when plans don't work out
- replacing something you borrowed and broke

So, between $300 and $500 is a great start. If you have a car, you might want to start with $500+, just in case.

Your Emergency Fund Needs Its Own Home

This is where many people fail. You see, while it is nice to have your emergency fund growing somewhere, it's more important that you have instant access to it, you know, in case of an emergency. So, if you can find an instant-access savings account that also allows you to grow your money, great; if not, always go for instant access. Another mistake people make is to stash their emergency fund with their current account. The problem here is that you can't really see what is part of your emergency fun and what isn't. And if you can't see that line, you will probably overspend.

You will want to open a separate savings account just for emergencies. Keeping this account separate from your main account will make it easier to track your savings and help you avoid dipping into your emergency fund for non-emergencies. Most banks will let you do this with the help of a parent or guardian. Some accounts offer better interest rates than others, so it's worth doing your research or asking your parent or guardian's advice on choosing the right account.

Building Your Safety Net

I mentioned that $300 to $400 might be a good start, but this doesn't mean you have to have $300 right away in your emergency fund. This is just a goal you should have and hopefully accomplish. The most important thing is consistency. Think of it like leveling up in a video game. You can actually divide it this way:

- Level 1: $100 saved
- Level 2: $250 saved
- Level 3: $500 saved

There's one last thing I want to address here. An emergency fund is not only for the paranoid. It's all about being prepared. When something goes wrong—and sooner or later, something will—you are ready for what comes, at least financially.

3

WISE SPENDING

Sometimes, money feels like it disappears faster than a Snapchat story. One minute, you're looking at your allowance or part-time salary, and the next minute, it's gone. I'm writing this chapter specifically for those who feel this happens every month. Also, I just want to make this clear: This is not a chapter on how to live your life as if you are broke all the time. It's about learning how to spend your money wisely.

Here, we will be looking at how you can go about buying the things you want and need without the sudden realization that your money is gone. In more detail, we will be looking at how you can:

- master the art of getting what you want without emptying your bank account.
- dodge those sneaky marketing traps.
- handle the awkward moments when your friends want to do something expensive.

- make smarter choices about when to spend and when to save.
- keep your social life alive without going broke.

NEEDS VS. WANTS: A GUIDE TO MINDFUL SPENDING

Let me begin this section with a story that might sound familiar to you. Let's call this teen John. Last month, he needed new shoes (his old ones were literally falling apart, so he's allowed to spend money on new ones, okay?). He was browsing online shops when he found these limited edition Jordans that all his favorite YouTubers were wearing (hard to say no, right?). The shoes he was looking for were about $60, but those Jordans were $200—a bit over three times the cost of the shoes he was looking for. John kept looking at his phone, not knowing what to do. Certainly, it is an internal battle we all know well.

Here's a funny thing about needs and wants: We often get confused about which is which. Sure, John needed shoes, but did he need the Jordans? No. So, that's a *want*. Did he need shoes? Absolutely yes. So, that's a *need*. Now, I know it's hard to think clearly when you have your wants right in front of you, but you can always step away, think it over, and come to a rational conclusion (which, in this case, would be the $60 shoes, just in case you were still wondering).

Making Room for Both

Now, I don't advocate for a boring life. I'm not telling you that you should never buy things for fun. Instead, I'm going to tell you about how to make room for both needs and wants without going broke.

If your money is a whole pizza, the biggest slice should go to needs (yes, the dull but more important stuff). However, you should still save a smaller slice for your wants. This could mean putting 70% of your money toward needs and splitting the remaining 30% between savings and wants. A quick example: If you get a $100 allowance, that's $70 for your needs, $15 for savings, and $15 for the fun stuff.

For the sake of finality, John ended up buying the $60 shoes and setting up a savings goal for the Jordans. By the time he reached his goal, the Jordans weren't trending anymore, and John realized he actually preferred a different style, which brings us to the next point we are about to discuss.

The Art of the Pause

I've mentioned this a couple of times, but these super simple tricks work wonders. Here's the gist: You see something you want to buy really bad; you wait 24 (or 48 for expensive stuff) hours and go back to it and see if you still want to buy it or not. More often than not, you won't want to buy it anymore. Your brain will come to its senses by then, and you will be able to see clearly.

There's actually an alternate method to this called the screenshot method. Whenever you see something you want to buy online, take a screenshot and add it to an album called something like, "Maybe Buy." After a couple of weeks, look at the album again, and you probably won't want 99% of the things you find there.

Track Your Spending

I know we've already talked briefly about tracking your spending, but here's an alternative way of doing it. Create a notes page (or, if you're old school, take out your notebook). Every single time you spend money, write it down. I mean *everything*, okay? At the end of each week, look back and label each purchase as either "needs" or "wants." I think you will be surprised by your findings. Most likely, you will find out that you spend way too much on wants, which is something you can work on and cut back on.

THE PSYCHOLOGY BEHIND IMPULSE BUYING AND HOW TO CONTROL IT

So, the main question in this section is quite simple, actually. Why do we buy stuff we don't need? Why do we need another mug when we already have six and only drink coffee twice a day? Why would we buy that limited edition hoodie and only wear it twice a year?

As always, I think it's better to explain concepts with a story first. Tyler was having a rough day after completely failing a math test. While scrolling through TikTok to feel better (I know), he saw this gaming keyboard that supposedly makes every player much better (but does it, really?). Believe it or not, there was a 30% flash sale on it, and only 2 hours left. How lucky for Tyler, right? Doesn't it seem like we are always bumping into a flash sale? Anyway, the "Buy Now" button was flashing, and Tyler couldn't resist. By the way, this is a classic impulse buy.

Should we be disappointed that Tyler bought it? Well, it was not his fault if he was unaware of the mechanics behind this marketing ploy. The thing is, our brains are wired in such a way that makes us impulse buy. When you're stressed, shopping gives you a quick mood boost. If you're bored, the "Add to Cart" button seems very tempting. Could he have done better? Sure. But he didn't know what I'm about to tell you.

Taking Control

How do we fight against marketing experts and our own brains? We have already talked about a couple of strategies: The 24-hour/48-hour wait or the screenshot strategy. They work wonders here.

But there's another thing I want to highlight: the real cost of impulse buying (which, by the way, goes beyond just money). Let's do some quick math. Say you impulse buy $20 a week (which is not that much, but you can do better). Maybe you find some random Amazon product, make in-app purchases, or get that Starbucks coffee. Let me just tell you that $20 a week equals $1,040 a year. What else could you buy with that money?

- a great gaming computer
- a decent start to your car fund
- a spring break trip with your friends

So, you tell me. Do you need that Amazon purchase? Is that spicy pumpkin latte worth it? Probably not. But it's more than money we're talking about here. Every time you impulse buy, you are allowing your brain to win. You're telling it that it's okay to not have self-control. The more you impulse buy, the worse it gets.

Turning Self-Control Into a Game

You can actually turn resisting impulsive buying into a fun game. You can create a, let's call it, "Temptation Tracker," and every time you resist an impulse, you get a point. Then, you can turn that point system into rewards:

- 5 points = small treat
- 10 points = medium reward
- 25 points = something bigger (but don't go overboard).

The important thing here is that by the time you get enough points for the biggest reward, you've already saved more money than the reward costs (again, unless you go overboard with it).

QUALITY VS. QUANTITY: SPENDING WISELY ON WHAT MATTERS

Do you remember the earbuds example? If you buy cheap $20 earbuds every two months, it gets more expensive than buying some good ones at $80. Well, this is the main focus of this section. When you're working with limited money, it's tempting to go for the cheapest option; however, as you know, sometimes, being "cheap" is more expensive.

The "Cost Per Use" Dilemma

We all have a piece of clothing that we love and wear quite often. Let's say it's a hoodie that cost you $50, and you've worn it 100 times. Essentially, every time you wore it, it cost you 50 cents. Now, compare that to a $15 fast-fashion hoodie you bought that fell apart after 5 wears. That would be $3 per use. A lot more expensive, right?

To calculate the cost per use:

- take the price of what you want to buy,
- divide it by how many times you'll realistically use it.

For example: Those $120 Nike Air Forces you will wear 200 times will equal 60 cents per wear, but those $20 knockoff pairs you will only wear 20 times will equal $1 per wear. Not great. This is just to show you that sometimes, the "expensive" is not that expensive after all.

When to Go Big and When to Go Budget?

Not everything needs to be top-shelf quality, so let's have a better look at what should and what shouldn't.

Let's begin with your phone. You should definitely invest in a good one. You can use it to study, connect with friends, manage your money apps, take pictures, and more. Now, do get one that does what it needs to do. If you can get one that costs $500 instead of $800 just because the latter has features you will never use, then go for the cheaper one. Do the math. How long do you think you will have it? Other things to spend good money on are probably a backpack, a good winter jacket, or a laptop. These are things that you need.

Now, where should you save your money? On a shirt you will wear once on a gig. Trendy accessories that will last as long as the trend itself (which these days is no more than a week, it seems). If you're experimenting with different styles or buying something for one specific occasion, fast fashion has its place, but you shouldn't regularly buy it.

The Sustainability Factor

How you spend affects more things than you might have imagined. All of these five-dollar t-shirts and hoodies often come with hidden costs to the environment and the people making them. Buying better quality means less waste, better working conditions for those making them, less money spent replacing things, and less time shopping for replacements.

How to Spot Quality

The first thing I always like to do is check the reviews. Don't just look at the star rating; actually read the reviews of the people who have used the product. Warranty does matter, even if it is something people often overlook. If a company stands behind its product with a good warranty, that's usually a good sign.

Of course, you can also ask friends or family who have used products you want to buy. There's no better review than from those you trust. And well, this probably goes without saying, but brand reputation is also an important factor.

UNDERSTANDING SALES AND MARKETING TRICKS

You're just scrolling down TikTok, and suddenly, you see those sneakers you were thinking about the day before. Coincidence? Not necessarily. Marketers have gotten really good (and sneaky) at knowing exactly when and how to catch your attention. You know those "Only one item left" warnings are sort of countdowns that make you feel like you're missing out? These are just marketers playing with your emotions and making you feel like you need to buy now or lose it forever. PS: There are always more.

How many "limited edition" items have you come across? To be honest, from a production point of view, having many "limited editions" is not advantageous for anyone because they cost more to make. I'm not saying some things might not be limited edition, but not everything is. The problem with these "fake" limited editions is the urge they give you. That's exactly what the marketers are after. Brands are absolute masters at making regular things seem special and ordinary prices feel like amazing deals. If you see a 50% off on a $100 shirt (now down to $50), wouldn't you think it's a great deal? Sure, but that $100 price tag never existed in the first place. Essentially, it's an illusion they create to make you buy more.

Critical Media Literacy

Let's do a quick exercise. Next time you're scrolling down a social media app, pay close attention to how different ads make you feel. Do you feel less confident because that skincare ad is pointing out a "problem" you have never noticed before? Or maybe you believe your current gaming setup is not cool enough after watching your favorite streamer.

Again, these are no accidents. They are carefully designed scenarios and ads to make you reach for your wallet. Understanding this is the way to break the spell and become a smarter consumer. It's not the easiest thing in the world; after all, companies spend millions studying exactly how to press your emotional buttons. But it's not something superhuman to achieve. All you need to recognize is the marketing triggers, and then you're off the hook.

The Role of Influencers

I hate to break to you, but you know your favorite YouTuber or streamer? They are not your friends, especially when it comes to recommendations. They are salespeople. Most of the products and services they advertise are because they got paid to. So, every time you consider buying something from an influencer, remember they're not spending their own money like you are.

Smart Consumer Tactics

Now you know their tricks, which means you can turn the tables and make sales work for you. Continue to populate that wishlist of things you actually want or need. When sales come around (and they will), you will know exactly what's worth buying and what's marketing hype. Remember: Black Friday, Cyber Monday, and end-of-season sales are all great ways to save money.

MONEY AND FRIENDSHIPS: HANDLING SOCIAL SPENDING PRESSURE

Oh, peer pressure can be an awful thing, but luckily, I have some experience and wisdom to give you. Say your friends are all heading to that new restaurant downtown after the game. Everyone's excited (your team won, of course), and everyone's getting fancy burgers and milkshakes (for that Insta pic). However, you've already spent most of your weekly allowance, and payday from your part-time job isn't until the end of next week. The truth is that your friends influence the way you spend money, even if you don't fully realize it. Maybe it's those new Jordans or the latest iPhone—sometimes, keeping up with the trends is not easy, especially if you have other goals.

When you show up at your friend's house, and they show you their new gaming console, your old one doesn't seem as fun, right? It's normal to feel this way; however, one thing you have to keep in mind is that everyone's financial situation is different. Some of your friends might have bigger allowances, or their parents might buy them more stuff. Others might be putting themselves into debt to keep up their appearances. But there's one thing you have to do, which we will see in the next section.

Setting Boundaries

It's absolutely fine to say no to spending money, especially if you don't have it. How do you do this without feeling like you're missing out or letting your friends down? Well, let me address the last first. If they are really your friends, they will understand, and they won't get mad. If they do, I'm sorry to tell you, but you need new friends. Now, let's get back to the first. Honesty is vital here. Don't make up excuses about why you can't go somewhere—be as straightforward as possible. Say that this place is a little out of your budget at the moment, and they will likely accommodate your needs (real friends will, anyway) because they want to spend time with you; it doesn't matter where.

Alternative Social Options

But who says you need to spend money to have fun with friends? Some of my best hangouts with friends cost me nothing or almost nothing. Instead of going to a restaurant, why not go for a picnic? If everyone brings something, you will have a feast, and, as a plus, you won't impulse buy anything.

If you like to play video games, you can game-share. Some games require only one of your friends to own in order for you to play together, or you can go for free-to-play games (there are some real gems). You can have some snacks while you play instead of ordering food.

Of course, these are just ideas. There's so much more you can do for almost nothing (monetarily); you just have to get creative.

Open Communication

You know, I didn't mention one thing when talking about being honest about money to your friends. More often than not, they will actually feel relieved because perhaps many of them are feeling the pressure, too, but they are just too embarrassed to tell anyone. Some of them might be going through some family finan-cial crisis; others might be saving for something big. There are a million reasons why, but you can be the one starting the conversation.

4

BANKING AND CREDIT BASICS

I still remember when my money solely lived in my piggy bank. Those were simpler times. I'm sure you remember that, too, but now you have an allowance or even a part-time job, and you can't keep stashing your money in a piggy bank under your bed. You need an actual bank and a bank account, of course.

Here's something that is probably true: No one ever taught your parents how banking worked, and they had to figure it all out, often through trial and error (which might have come with some expensive mistakes). Now, you don't have to go through that. You have them—and for a more in-depth understanding—you have this book, particularly this chapter, to teach you how banking works.

We will be looking at how you can pick the best possible bank for you (one without hidden fees); how credit works (and I know you've probably heard some not-so-nice things about it, but I'm ready to change your mind); and also about credit scores. But I don't want to overwhelm you with all of this, so let's just get started with picking your first bank.

CHOOSING YOUR FIRST BANK ACCOUNT

Even if not right now, at some point in the near future, you will have to move your cash from under the pillow and place it some-where else—ideally, in a bank account. But how do you do that? Do you walk down to the bank or do it online? What type of bank and account do you need to get? Let's break this into parts.

First, let's talk about the different bank account options, starting with a checking account. This is the bank account your part-time paycheck goes to and where you withdraw money if you need it. The best feature of a checking account is that your money is always accessible as long as you have a debit card that comes with the account. A debit card is like a credit card but linked to your checking account, so you can only spend what you have in there.

Then, there's the savings account, which is what you use to stash your money that you don't need to use immediately. Here, your money grows simply by letting it be there. This should also be the account where you leave your money for all your goals. Your money grows because of interest that we already talked about; however, more often than not, this is simple interest and not compound, but there are exceptions.

Also, just for your information, some banks offer student or teen accounts, which are just like regular checking accounts but with fewer fees, lower minimum balances, and other perks.

Evaluating Bank Services

As you might imagine, not all banks are exactly the same. The first thing I recommend checking is their app. You'll likely use their banking app far more than visiting a branch, so having a reliable one is essential. Look for features like mobile check deposits, easy money transfers, and customizable notifications. Of course, don't forget to review fees—maintenance, overdraft, or ATM fees. Ideally, you'd avoid these entirely, but depending on the other perks, you might decide some fees are worth it.

Even if we live in the digital world, the location of physical branches is still important and something you should consider when looking for your first bank. There will be times when you might want to talk to a person face-to-face, so the location of the branch is important. Also, make sure they have good customer service in case you need to call them to solve any issues.

Opening Your Account

When you pick the bank and checking account you want, you have to actually open it. Most banks ask for the same things. If you are under 18, you will need a parent or guardian to open the account with you, and this will be a "joint account." This simply means the adult who opens the account with you knows what you're doing with the account. Yes, I know, but this is the only way to get an account if you're under 18.

You will need your ID or driver's license if you already have it, your social security number, and proof of address (which, even if you're over 18 but still live with your parents, they can help you with). Many banks let you start the process online but may want an in-person appointment to finish the process.

The process itself is pretty straightforward. You just need to fill out some forms, make a deposit (which is usually quite low), and set up your online banking.

Managing Your Account

Download the online banking app right away because you will often be managing your account from there. These are quite simple to use, and I suggest you set up notifications so you know when your money is leaving your account or when you receive it. When it comes to depositing money, if you earn from your part-time job, you will have to give your bank details to your employer, and they will send them directly to your account. If you want to add cash to your account, you can use a bank's ATM (they can be found inside the bank, but they are most often found outside the bank as drive-up or walk-up stations, as well as independent locations such as grocery stores, malls, or convenience stores).

CREDIT CARDS FOR TEENS: WHAT YOU NEED TO KNOW

Okay, so let's talk about credit cards—I can almost hear the panic emanating from you. Let me just say, they are not as bad as people say. I mean, don't get me wrong; if you overuse them and have no control, they can bring problems. But if you use them wisely, they can bring you many benefits.

The way it works is quite simple: The bank gives you a brand-new card with a limit (for example, $2,500), and you can use the card up to that limit whenever you want. Now, you don't have to (and shouldn't) spend the whole amount. You should only use the credit card if you know you can pay it back by the due date. If you aren't able to pay it off, you will incur interest, and often, these are high-interest rates.

In the event that you make a big purchase with a credit card because you have to, like paying to get your car fixed (if you have an emergency fund, this will be covered!)—and you can't pay the entire balance in a month, you can still pay it off over time. Be sure to pay more than the minimum each month (set by the bank depending on how much you owe and the interest on your card) because if you only pay the minimum, you will be in debt for a long time, and that debt will only continue to grow.

Benefits and Risks of Using Credit Cards

When it comes to their benefits, credit cards are excellent tools to build your credit score. This is like a financial report card that will matter when you take out loans or a mortgage. If you are a responsible credit card user by paying on time and not maxing it out, you are building a good financial reputation.

As I've explained above, a credit card can also be really convenient, but there's more to it. If you're shopping online, it's preferable to do it with a credit card because they have better fraud protection.

But let me highlight this again: There are risks. It's way too easy to overspend when your money is not on the line (meaning you don't see it leaving your checking account right away). An attitude of "I'll pay it back later" can have consequences and lead to some serious debt, and at times, negatively impact your financial reputation.

Choosing Your First Credit Card

You want something reliable that won't potentially give you a lot of trouble (it is still a credit card, though). Since you are a teen, chances are you will probably have to start with a secured credit card or become an authorized user on your parent's card. A secured credit card is like a training credit card; you put down a deposit (say $1,000), and that's your credit limit.

But if you already put the money upfront, why use a credit card, then? By paying off the amount you spend every month, you build your credit score. When looking at credit cards, don't fall for the great marketing some banks use. Focus on a few key things:

- no annual fee
- low interest rate
- simple rewards
- good mobile app and account alerts

These are the most important things you should have with your first credit card. Anything else might make it too complicated and unnecessary.

Responsible Usage

Once you've got your first credit card, how do you use it responsibly? Well, treat it like real money. At the end of the day, it is. Why would you buy something with a credit card if you don't have the money to pay it right now?

Set up automatic payments for at least the minimum amount due; however, always try to pay more and aim to pay it in full every month. Missing a payment is bad for your report, and it will stay there for years to come.

Keep your balance low. Often, more than 30% of credit utilization (30% of the credit limit) reflects badly on your credit score, but aim for much less (DeNicola, 2016). Also, keep an eye on your account and set up alerts for every single purchase, just in case. With that, checking your statement every month will help you stay on top of things.

Credit Scores: How They Work and Why They Matter

I know I've just mentioned briefly how credit scores work, but I think we need to go more in-depth about the topic. You could compare it to your GPA, but this one follows you your whole life. It's essentially a number between 300 and 850 that tells everyone in the financial world how good you are at handling money. And, of course, the higher the number, the better.

But this "financial GPA" tracks many different things. Let's have a look at these factors.

Payment history is much like your school attendance, and it counts for the most points (35% of your credit score). Every time you pay a bill on time, you are on track, but if you miss a payment, your credit score will suffer. There's credit utilization, which tells you how much of your credit card limit you've used, and it's the next most important factor because it accounts for 30% of your score.

The length of credit history accounts for 15% of your credit score, and it has to do with the length of time you've had credit card accounts open. So, even if you have a credit card that you don't use, don't close the account because it can give you some points on your credit score. The last 20% is your mix of credit types and new credit card applications. The more diversity you have in terms of credit, the better credit cards, car loans, mortgages, and other financial things you will have access to. But keep in mind that you need to be able to pay them.

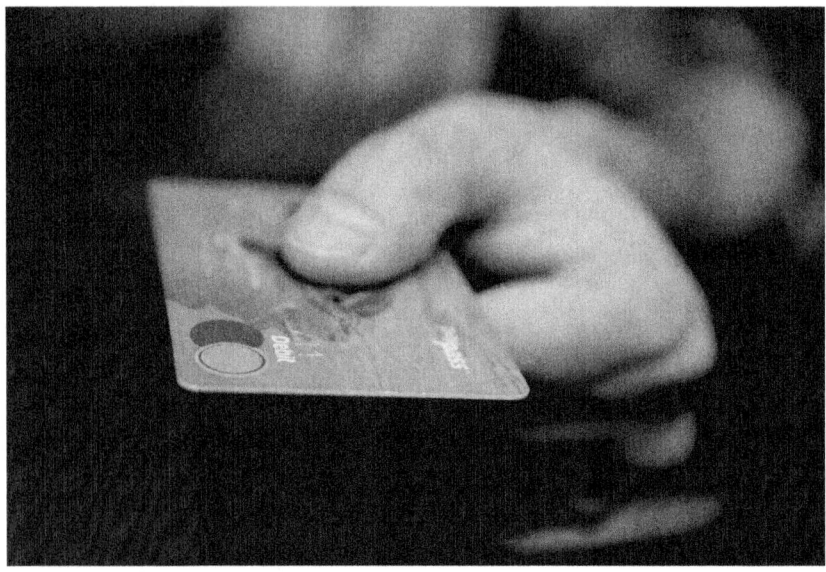

Building a Good Credit Score

Now you know what makes up a credit score, but how exactly do you get a good one? Well, the first thing you have to think about is actually having credit. Without it, you can't have a credit score. As I said before, become an authorized user on your parent's credit card. This will all you to start small and benefit from their good credit history. When you own a credit card, remember the payment due dates; they are very important.

Start slow; there's no rush, and obviously, you don't want to start spending without having the money to pay the balance back.

I can't emphasize enough the impact of your credit score. If you want a car, you will likely need a loan, which means you need a good credit score to borrow enough and still have good interest rates. This is true for personal loans, mortgages, and even renting an apartment (even though, when you rent, you don't need to borrow money).

PROTECTING YOURSELF FROM IDENTITY THEFT

Have you ever been scrolling Instagram and got a weird notification that someone just tried to buy $100 worth of things from across the world using your debit card, and you panicked because you didn't know what was going on? Well, that's identity theft. However, there are ways to prevent this.

What Is Identity Theft?

Identity theft can happen to anyone and in many different scenarios. It could be your debit card, family account details, or social security number. All of these and more are targeted by thieves who pretend to be you. Truth be told, teens are more likely to be targeted because they tend to share more online and are not as attentive to their accounts as adults are.

Think of the teens who share everything online, from their address to their birthday to their pet's name (which might be their password, too). All of this information might be important to these thieves.

Keeping the Bad Guys Out

I'm sure you've heard that using strong passwords is important, and it actually is. Don't use your dog's name and your birthday.

Instead, you can use your favorite song lyrics but turn it into an actual password. You know, instead of an "s," use a $, or instead of an "e," use a 3. Those sorts of things.

When It All Goes Wrong

Despite all the security you have implemented, the bad guys can still get hold of your information. Try not to panic, though I understand this is easier said than done. The first thing you should do is tell your parents (or guardian). I know you might not want to tell them you might have done something wrong, but you still have. Trust me, it's for the best, and they have legal power.

Call the bank right away because they can freeze your account quickly. Most banks have zero-liability policies, which means you will get your money back if someone steals it. Be sure to document everything. Screenshot suspicious activities, write down when you noticed the issue, and save any weird email the thief might have sent you. This is vital because you will need to file a police report.

Do You Need Identity Protection Services?

The simple answer is that they are quite useful. They can monitor your account, alert you to suspicious activity, and even clean up the mess if something goes wrong. However, they come at a cost. Usually between $10 and $30 a month. Keep in mind, however, that chances are that your bank offers basic identity protection for free. It might not be as comprehensive, but it is something. There are other things you can add to this, such as setting up alerts on your account, checking your account regularly, and being super smart when it comes to sharing your personal details online.

USING TECHNOLOGY TO MANAGE YOUR MONEY

You already spend a big part of your day on your phone, so what better than using it to manage your money, right?

Your Phone: Your Money Command Center

Your phone alone is not very useful when it comes to managing your money; you need good apps. YNAB and Mint are great for tracking where your money goes. You can connect them to your bank account, so everything is automated. They can even tell you if you spend too much money on dining out and what restaurant you spend more in. Plus, many of these types of apps are gamified, which means that they actually look like games with challenges and all of that. Qapital, for instance, lets you set your own rules, such as "save $5 every time I tweet" or rounding up your Starbucks order and sending that money to your savings.

Your Bank's Secret Powers

Of course, your regular online banking app is the center of it all. And, best of all, it also has some nice features you can use. Besides mobile depositing (taking a picture of your check to deposit it) and setting up notifications that we already talked about, it can also set up automatic payments for bill payments so you will never miss one.

But you can't just download every single financial app you see in the app store. You have to be mindful of security risks. Remember the phishing scams and all of that? That's how they happen. Two-factor identification is one of the best tools out there to guarantee the safety of your money. Also, free Wi-Fi can actually be pretty dangerous, so don't log into your financial apps with public Wi-Fi, as you don't know who's lurking. Also, it should go without saying that you should update your apps because they often fix security issues.

The Future Is Wild, and It's Already Here

I'm sure you've heard of cryptocurrencies and blockchain. No, I'm not going to deep dive into these topics or even convince you to buy them, but what I will say is that the technology behind it can actually change the way we look at money. In fact, many of the things we already use emerged from these technologies, such as digital wallets like Apple Pay or Google Pay. And this is already happening; in the future, who knows what we will be able to do? Take Venmo, for example, where you can send money with just text.

Well, the future is here, but there are many different things that will happen. Maybe you will be able to pay by scanning your face or using virtual reality to manage your investments. How cool would that be? The point is that technology makes things easier, especially when it comes to being smart about your money. You have all the tools right in your pocket, so use them wisely.

5

INTRODUCTION TO INVESTING

Now, we are getting into a topic that I'm sure you will enjoy, even if you think it's too complex. By the way, this is a myth —basic investment is not complicated at all, and with the tools we have today, you can start investing from your phone.

Investing lets you own a small part of your favorite brands. Yes, I'm talking Nike, Netflix, Tesla, Spotify, Nintendo, Apple, and many more. I'm not talking about owning their products (which you probably already do); I mean actual pieces of the company itself. The goal is for those pieces of the companies you own (called shares) to grow in value, just like the ultra-rare Magic: The Gathering card you bought as a kid that has now tripled in price. In time, if your shares increase in value, you can sell them for a lot more money.

That's the gist of investing: buy lower and sell higher. And investing is no longer just for rich people. As I've mentioned, many apps allow you to simply invest from your phone. Apps like Robinhood are quite popular among young investors. Often, these apps require very minimal investment (some as low as $1), and, in most cases, there are no fees. Just like compound interest, the sooner you start, the more you can earn.

So, this chapter is fully dedicated to investing and teaching you the basics so you can start right away.

INVESTING 101: UNDERSTANDING STOCKS, BONDS, AND MUTUAL FUNDS

Let's get right into it with a scenario. Say you got a share of Netflix just before the first *Stranger Things* dropped. When more people subscribed to the platform because of the success of the show, the company made more money, and so the value of your share increased. But if you'd bought Netflix shares just before they cracked down on password sharing, you would have seen a decrease in the value of your share (although later on, this was actually beneficial to the company).

Some companies like to share their profits with their shareholders (people who have shares of the company). This is called a dividend, which is usually paid every three months, and the amount you receive depends on the dividend payout of the company and the number of shares you have. That money goes straight to you, and you can either withdraw it or reinvest it. Word of advice: Unless you have a lot of shares from that company, the best course of action is to reinvest that dividend money into the stock.

Bonds: Lending Money to Get More Money Back

To simplify this, let's say you lend $20 to your friend, and they promise to pay back $22 the next day. This is essentially how bonds work, except you're not getting your money back that quickly. With bonds, you are lending your money to companies and the government (often local government). One of the benefits of bonds compared to stocks is that they are often safer, meaning you are more likely to get your money back on a specific date. Keep in mind that government bonds are even safer than company bonds because they almost never default. A default happens when the issuer of the bond (company or government) doesn't have the money to pay you back by the deadline. However, compared to stocks, bonds—especially government bonds—often provide lower returns.

Mutual Funds: Pooling Money

What if I tell you that you don't have to pick individual stocks or bonds? Instead, you can buy them in bundles. That's what mutual funds are. When you invest in a mutual fund, your money is pooled with other investors' money, and the fund buys shares from different companies. When you buy a share of the mutual fund, you're investing in many companies at once, which is much cheaper than buying them separately. Another benefit is that mutual funds are managed by professional investors. So, while you don't really have a say when it comes to which stocks you want in your basket, you have a professional picking stock and managing the pool of money the best they can. This is a great way to diversify your investments, which we will discuss later (great strategy, by the way).

There's a negative side to mutual funds: You have to pay the professional investor. They often collect their fee by taking a percentage of what the mutual fund makes. This is where exchange-traded funds (ETFs) come in to add more depth to your potential investment choices. ETFs are a lot like mutual funds, with only a few differences. First, they can be bought as shares straight from the stock market. They are also pooled investments from different investors, and buying a share from one gives you access to a diverse array of individual stocks. While ETFs are still managed, they are not actively managed (passively managed, instead) like mutual funds are, and so there are usually no management fees associated with them. There are a wide variety of EFTs available, from those focused on specific industries or strategies to ones covering almost any niche imaginable. A popular example is the S&P 500, which tracks the 500 largest companies on the New York Exchange. By buying one share of the S&P 500, you are buying tiny fractions of those 500 companies.

Diversification is one of the best strategies you can use when investing. Essentially, it comes down to the saying, "Don't put all your eggs in the same basket." Diversification in stocks means not putting all your money in one stock. In fact, you should diversify even more by not investing everything into one specific industry (like technology) or focusing just on stocks (for example, adding bonds to your investments).

To explain why, let's say you have all your money in Apple stocks, and they release the new iPhone, but it kind of stinks. Apple shares value will go down, and so will all your money. But if you have your money in Apple, Microsoft, McDonalds, and Nike, and only the Apple stock goes down, your overall investment doesn't go as down because you have the other stocks to balance it out, at least until Apple comes back up. Sometimes, industry-wide issues occur, such as the internet bubble of 2000 (Hayes, 2024). You're probably too young to remember, but there was a "bubble" that burst (it doesn't really matter what this means for now; we will get to it later), and all the technology sector companies lost a lot of value. This can happen to any industry, and that's why diversifying is important. As I've mentioned, diversifying outside the stock market is also important, so if the stock has a bad day, week, or month (yes, they have that sometimes), you don't lose your money.

Picking Your Investment Style

Everyone has their style, both in life and as investors (surprising, I know). Which one will be yours? Let's break down the different types of investment vehicles we've talked about.

Stocks are considered high-risk with a potential high return. Bonds are considered low-risk and low-return. Mutual funds, and I guess we can put ETFs here, too, are a mix of risk and rewards. I would pick an aggressive strategy (which would imply a lot of individual stocks) to start by having a mixed bag of everything. You are young, and time is your best ally when investing. Let's go into greater detail about investment styles.

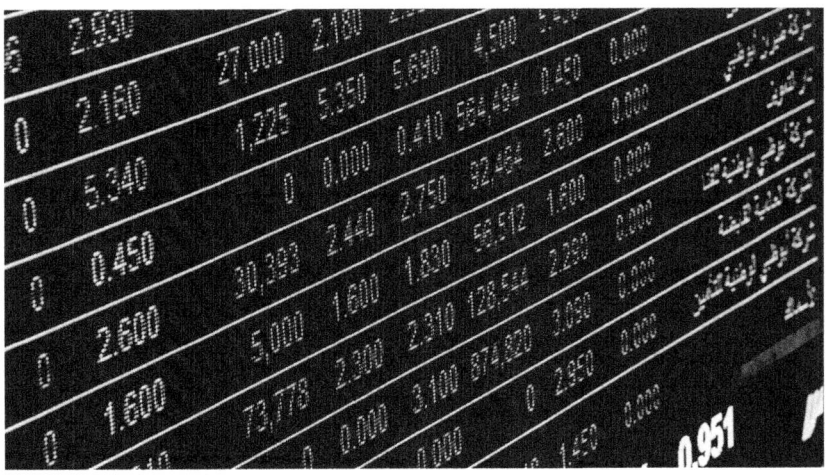

RISK VS. REWARD: FINDING WHAT INVESTMENT STYLE SUITS YOU

Investment styles come down to how you want to invest your money. It's pretty much like buying expensive sneakers and pondering if or when they are going to be out of style in the next few months.

The Risk-Reward Relationship

I gave you a little introduction to this relationship in the last part of the section above, but there's more that you need to consider. You know when Minecraft was what everyone was playing? If you bought shares of the company that made the game before it exploded, you would have made some serious money. But what if you bought shares at the peak of its popularity? Chances are you would have lost money. These are the basics of how risk-reward works. The bigger the potential reward, the bigger the risk and you can choose between low, medium, and high risk.

Low-risk strategies are mostly bonds because they are relatively safe, but the earnings are not that big. You could just leave it in your savings account if you want to be super, super safe. Medium risk is buying mutual funds, ETFs, and large company stocks like Nike, Apple, and Microsoft. High risk is investing in brand-new tech startups or cryptocurrency. You could either double your money or lose it all.

Finding Your Risk Tolerance

Risk tolerance is what we call the amount of money you are willing to lose or how well you handle uncertainty. Some people panic more than others because some have more to lose, which is fine. This also has to do with how much faith and patience you have. The stock market is unpredictable in a predictable way. If you have faith in one particular company and you know it is going to be worth investing in in the long term (say 5-10 years), you won't care if the stock price is down today because you have faith it will be all the way up there in the next few years.

If losing $50 in the stock market makes you lose sleep, then you are better off playing safe. But if you don't mind the stock values going up and down as long as they grow over time, then you are ready for the mix approach of stocks and bonds.

The Time Factor

Time is perhaps the most important factor. You are young and relatively inexperienced in the stock market, which means you shouldn't try to be a day trader (those who buy and sell stocks on a daily basis to capitalize on small stock movements). Think: When do you need the money you are investing? This money should be for the future—for college tuition, a car, or a down payment on an apartment. So, at this moment, your time horizon is long-term (or at least it should be). But let's break down your goals relative to investment horizons.

Short-term goals (1-3 years)

- Saving for a car, a trip with friends, a gaming setup
- Stick to safer investments because you don't want the market to crash and then you have no money when needed.

Medium-term goals (3-5 years)

- College tuition, potentially starting a business
- You can take some risks, but keep it balanced.

Long-term goals (5+ years)

- Saving for something in the future (for example, a downpayment for a house)
- You can afford to take some risks because you have time on your side to recover.

Choosing Your Investment Strategy

Based on your risk tolerance and time horizon, chances are you fall within one of these three strategy types:

- Conservative: You mostly invest in bonds and savings and maybe some high-quality stocks. 70% bonds; 30% stocks.
- Moderate: You invest in a mix of stocks and bonds. 60% stocks; 40% bonds.
- Aggressive: You invest mostly in stocks from emerging businesses and cryptocurrencies. 80-90% stocks; 10-20% bonds.

THE ROLE OF REAL ESTATE IN PERSONAL FINANCE

I haven't told you about something that is definitely going to excite you. And no, once again, real estate is not only for rich folks—well, at least not the type we are going to talk about. I'm not saying buying a mansion; I'm talking about investing in real estate with something called real estate investment funds (REITs).

Let's take a step back for a second here. You know when you go to the mall and you see all of those stores? Every single store is paying rent. Someone owns that space and is renting it out to stores, just like landlords make money by renting out their properties to tenants. All of these are real estate investments. Again, I'm not saying you have to buy an apartment. This is where REITs come in. They are just like stocks; in fact, they are more like ETFs. REITs allow you to invest in real estate without having to purchase a property outright. And just like stocks, you can start with $10. When you buy a share of a REIT, you usually buy several tiny parts of different real estate or properties.

Making Money While You Sleep

You buy REITs just like you buy stocks. The interesting thing is that REITs have to give shareholders the majority of their profit, which means you are paid dividends, often every month. While they might not appreciate in value as much as stocks—since they are distributing most of their profits—you still get it in the form of dividends, which you can then reinvest to grow your wealth even more. This makes REITs an appealing option for a steady stream of income.

Now, let's leave the stock market aside for a moment. Real estate is often seen as a solid, long-term investment, but it does come with a high entry cost. Typically, you need to buy property, which can be expensive, especially in a competitive housing market. However, once you own a property, you are basically making money in your sleep once you rent it out.

When Things Go Wrong

If you buy a property to rent, you become a landlord. This often means you are responsible for making sure the property is in good condition to be rented out. There are times when you might have to fix some things around the house or even get a call at 3 a.m. because the water heater broke down, which you might have to pay for. While property often goes up with time, and you can sell it at a higher price than you bought it years before, there can be issues like the house price crash of 2008 (again, you might be too young to remember). Essentially, there was a house price crisis, many houses lost value, and a lot more bad things happened to the economy. Anyway, it's a good investment, but it has its issues like everything else.

Real Estate vs. Stocks

Well, there's no correct answer. At this point in your life, I would invest in REITs (obviously, you might not have the means to buy a property just yet), and it is another great way to diversify your investment portfolio.

But there's a lot to learn about real estate investment, and, of course, you can start right now. Websites like Zillow let you see a lot of information about houses, such as prices, and there are many things you can start getting familiar with.

Here's another fancy word for you: liquidity. This is all about how fast you can get money in your hand if you were to sell your investments (because life can be unpredictable, and we might need money fast). While stocks (REITs included) are relatively quick in this regard and so highly liquid, actual real estate investments like properties are highly illiquid. If you need money quickly and have to sell your property to get it, you might be in trouble. First, you need to sell the house, which takes time in itself, and then with all the bureaucracy on top of it... let's just say it takes a long time. So, this is also something to consider when investing.

GETTING STARTED WITH SIMPLE INVESTMENTS

Alright, now you know quite a bit about investments, but how exactly do you start? Well, you just start. As I've mentioned, you don't need a gazillion dollars; if you have $10 or $20, that's good enough.

Taking Your First Steps Into Investing

Like with everything in life, you want to start simple, right? Get to know how everything works until you get enough confidence to take the next step. The first thing you have to look at is somewhere to actually make your investments. This is called a brokerage account, which might sound super "adult," but there are many teenage-friendly brokerage accounts. One app used by many young investors like you is Robinhood or Acorns. If you're under 18, you still need your parents or guardian to help you set up a custodial account, just like with a bank account. While it is still your money, you "need" a supervisor until you are 18. It's not ideal, but it shouldn't be a problem.

Start Micro-Investing

Many apps, such as Acorns, let you start investing with literally spare change. Say you buy a $4.50 Starbucks coffee, and Acorns round it up to $5. That extra 50 cents goes to an investment of your choice. That's pretty cool, right? Robinhood works a little differently. You have to fund your account from your bank account and invest in whatever you want. It's not micro-investing, but you can begin with very little money as well.

Just a little note to those who might want to get a financial advisor: I wouldn't recommend it at this point, and here's why. First, you probably can't afford to pay for one right now, and if you can, they might take a significant portion of your investment money, which isn't worth it when you're just starting out. Financial advisors can be helpful, but their services tend to be more beneficial for people with larger investment portfolios who need more complex advice. For now, it's better to focus on building your savings and learning the basics of investing on your own.

However, if you are set on speaking with a financial advisor, look for one who specializes in working with younger investors and is "fee-only." This means they'll charge you directly for their time rather than taking a portion of your investment. This setup ensures their advice is unbiased and based on your needs, not how much they can earn from your investment.

Setting Realistic Investment Goals

You've probably heard stories about investors who became millionaires in one day because they "bet" everything on one stock that exploded. Well, I'm sorry to disappoint you, but this almost never happens (it can happen, but it is very unlikely). That's why you should set up some realistic investment goals.

Let me give you some examples of different types of realistic investment goals:

- Short-term goal (1 year): Save and invest $500.
- Medium-term goal (3-4 years): Build up $5,000 for college expenses.

- Long-term goal (10+ years): Invest to build a down payment for a future house.

Oh, and you can use SMART goals for this, of course. It makes it a lot easier. Also, make sure you align your goals with your financial aspirations and risk tolerance.

CRYPTOCURRENCY: A TEEN'S GUIDE TO DIGITAL MONEY

Crypto seems to be everywhere, and sometimes not for the right reasons. Let me tell you right away that the crypto market, at this point, is far more unregulated than the stock market, and so there are more risks. The fact that it is more volatile than other markets also suggests more risks but also higher rewards.

What's Cryptocurrency?

Well, the money in your bank account is really just a bunch of numbers, right? Most of us don't even use cash anymore; we just tap away with our cards or phones. Cryptocurrency is sort of like that, with the exception that it is not controlled by any government. But, much like money and Magic: The Gathering Cards, faith that something has value counts. There are countless cryptocurrencies nowadays, and the most popular of them all (and also the first one to really break out) is Bitcoin. It all began back in 2009 when someone (or some people) called Satoshi Nakamoto (no one knows who he or they are; isn't that fascinating?) created Bitcoin (Tidy, 2024). Essentially, they created digital money that works without the need for banks. Since then, thousands of other cryptocurrencies have emerged, each with its own feature; many (and this is important) are scams, so pay close attention and do your research before investing in one (not Bitcoin, that's legit).

The Tech Behind It

More important than the cryptocurrency itself is perhaps the mechanics behind it. With a technology called blockchain—for simplicity, think of this as a giant digital diary that everyone can see, but no one can change. Every transaction ever made is there, forever, unchanged. If you send Bitcoin to a friend, everyone can see it, but there are no names, so you don't really know who's who.

You might be wondering why people think this is secure. Well, some math problems are pretty complicated, right? Every time there's a transaction in the blockchain, computers (not people, we couldn't do that) have to solve a very, very, but like, *very* hard math problem to verify the transaction. This is called mining (but it has nothing to do with actual mining; don't fret—it's just a name). And so, these computers essentially make sure no one cheats.

Of course, things are a little more complex, but for the sake of understanding and to eventually get started on cryptocurrencies, you don't need every detail of how everything works behind the scenes.

Getting Into the Crypto Game

Let me emphasize this once again: crypto is volatile, so make sure you fully understand it before investing in it. Here's my take if you're thinking about investing in crypto. Start small, like $10, $20 small. Only invest money that you can afford to lose. Use legitimate exchanges like Coinbase. If anyone promises you to get you rich quickly, run away; it's a lie. And, of course, do your research. As I've mentioned, Bitcoin and Ethereum are legit, but they are also volatile.

What's Next?

So, what's next? What does the future hold? No one knows for certain, but is the future of money digital? Most likely. Well, it kind of already is, and I'm sure cryptocurrencies or, at least, its underlying technology will be a part of it. Just look at how money has changed in the past 10 or 15 years. Your parents didn't have Venmo, Apple Pay, and absolutely no crypto. They used mainly cash, and debit cards were around, of course, but it wasn't that widespread.

The best way to get ready for the future is to closely follow what is happening in the financial world. Read, research, and experiment (safely). The future is already happening; we just don't know where exactly it is going.

Also, if you want to learn more in-depth about investments, check the other book in the series called: *Investing For Teenagers Made Simple: Your Step-By-Step Path to Obtaining Wealth and Financial Freedom Quickly.*

MAKE A DIFFERENCE WITH YOUR REVIEW!!!!

"People who give without expectation live longer, happier lives and make more money."

— FREDDIE MERCURY

Hey there! Do you ever wonder how you can make a difference, even when you're just chilling at home? Well, here's your chance!

Would you lend a hand to someone you've never met, even if you didn't get a pat on the back for it?

Our mission is to make "Money Skills and Personal Finance For Teens Made Easy: Your Step-By-Step Guide to Budgeting, Saving and Investing that will develop smart Money Habits and Unlock Financial Freedom for Life" accessible to every teenager. Seriously, everything I do comes back to that mission. And guess what? I need your help to make it happen.

Most folks do judge a book by its cover (and its reviews). So, here's my ask on behalf of all those teenagers out there struggling with financial literacy, understanding investing, and just generally feeling lost in the money maze:

Could you take a moment to leave a review for this book?

Your review is like a small gift. It costs nothing and takes less than a minute, but it could change a fellow teenager's life forever. Your review could help someone start a business, support their family, find meaningful work, or even help them in a direction to get their dream home.

So, if you're up for spreading some good vibes and making a difference, all you have to do is leave a review. It's as simple as that!

Just scan the QR code below to leave your review:

If you're down with helping out a fellow teenager, you're totally my kind of person. Welcome to the club!

And guess what? I'm super pumped to help you achieve financial independence, accumulate wealth, and gain confidence in managing your money faster than you can imagine. Get ready for some awesome strategies coming your way in the next chapters.

Thanks a bunch from the bottom of my heart. Now, let's get back to our regularly scheduled program!

Your biggest fan,

Riley Wealth

PS - Fun fact: Sharing something valuable with someone else makes you even more valuable to them. So, if you think this book can help another struggling teenager, why not pass it along?

6

EARNING YOUR OWN MONEY

I f you get an allowance, you probably remember the first time you received it, right? Do you remember the feeling? I'll venture to say you probably found it exhilarating. Now, if you increase your excitement by a few levels, that's how it feels to earn your own money. Your age is the perfect time to start earning some money. Even though you might think you are just a teenager with no experience, let me tell you that the world is full of opportunities for you to earn money.

Maybe you are great in a particular subject, and you can teach it for money. Or maybe you have an artistic side, and, well, there's so much you can do with that. Maybe even your gaming addiction can bring you some cash through tournaments or streaming. These are just some suggestions, but in this chapter, we will get to how you can do all of these things.

We'll look at everything from traditional part-time jobs (and how to get hired) to starting your own business. But more importantly, we will be focusing on opportunities that fit into your already busy school life.

PART-TIME JOBS: FINDING WORK AS A TEEN

So, from all the possibilities you have, you decided that a part-time job is the way to go, and that's awesome. You not only get money (obviously), but you will also get to work in a real working environment where you can get loads of experience.

Where to Find Your First Job?

If your parents tell you to just walk into the store and hand over your resume, tell them that this is no longer the early 2000s, and things work a little differently. While your local business still hires teens, they probably won't advertise it on the window. The retail stores at the mall are a great place to get your first job, but you also have fast food restaurants, movie theaters (a favorite of mine), and seasonal gems like summer jobs.

Now, pick up your phone and download Indeed and Snagajob. These apps allow you to filter and find jobs that are more appropriate to you. There are companies that also accept applications through their website, so keep an eye out.

Building Your First Resume

It doesn't matter if you don't have experience; you probably have more than you think. Are you the captain of a team in school? Or have you organized any events? Or do you run a YouTube channel? These are all great skills you can add to your resume. Let's have a look at what a resume should have:

- your contact info (and if you have a funny email address, create a new, more professionally sounding one)
- your school and GPA

- activities you're involved in
- any leadership positions you've occupied
- special skills (you could be tech-savvy, bilingual, or simply great with people. Add that in)

Nailing the First Interview

Interviews don't necessarily have to be scary. In fact, they are usually quite friendly and more like having a conversation than an interrogation. Think of them as an opportunity to introduce yourself and learn more about the company and role. The interviewer probably knows you're new to the job market, so they don't expect years of experience, but they do want to see that you're eager and prepared. There are a few common questions you might be asked, and while some can feel tricky, they are just a way for the interviewer to get to know you better. These include questions like:

- Why do you want to work here?
- How do you handle busy situations?
- Can you tell me about yourself? (definitely the hardest one)

One of the most important things to remember, regardless of the position you are applying for, is your attire. While it's important to dress professionally, you don't need to overdo it. Keep it simple and neat to show that you care about making a good impression.

Balancing Work and Life

Now, this is the real challenge. Having a job while you're still studying can be a little overwhelming, and to have both going smoothly, you need to strategize. Most places hiring students know that school comes first, but you need to be upfront about your schedule.

You can start with just a few hours, like 10 or 15 a week, and see how it goes from there. You can use your phone's calendar to block out time for classes (and homework!), any extracurricular activities, work shifts, and, of course, free time. And, if your grades are slipping or you're just too tired all the time, you can cut back on some hours at work; that's totally fine.

FROM PASSION TO PROFIT: TURNING HOBBIES INTO CASH

Sometimes, you come across things on your social feed, and you stop to think, *Hold on, people actually pay for this*? This could be graphic t-shirts, mugs, coming up with viral TikTok dances, or any artsy projects.

Finding Your Money-Making Thing

The best way to start is by thinking about what you are already good at—you know, the things you enjoy doing for fun when you should be doing your homework. Those are not random skills but business opportunities.

The best part of turning your hobby into a business is that you already love to do it. For instance, there are people out there who would pay for the digital art you make in your spare time. The gaming skills could be used to create tutorials for other players on YouTube.

Turning Your Hobby Into a Side Hustle

When it comes to turning your hobbies into money, it's all about finding the right angle. Take gaming, for example. Instead of just playing it, think about how you could show others how to play. If it's art, what makes your style unique?

As with everything, you should start slow and gradually build up an audience. If you're great at makeup, you can begin with friends and family and see how it goes from there. You can eventually offer tutorials on Instagram.

Getting Your Work Out There

Now, this is something that you will eventually have to do if you want to earn money. I'm sure you already know the ins and outs of social media, but you have to put those skills into practice. Instagram Stories are a great way to do this and showcase your work in progress. TikTok is amazing for giving potential customers a sneak peek behind the scenes. YouTube could be a place for tutorials and longer videos.

One other thing you need to think about is bringing authenticity to your work. This is what brings people in. Your own take, your own way of doing things. People connect with real people, so don't try to be someone else.

Also, the platforms you choose to sell your stuff also matter; they have to be in line with what you are offering. Anything physical you can sell is better posted on a marketplace like Etsy. For digital services, Upwork or Fiverr are great places.

The Boring Stuff

While boring, this stuff is important. Once you start making money, you will be entering the world of business, which means taxes and other legal stuff are involved. If you're under 18, you will need the support of your parents or guardian for some of these things. We already talked about this, but make sure you keep good records from the very start. You can either use your phone or a spreadsheet but have something that can help you track earnings and expenses.

THE GIG ECONOMY: OPPORTUNITIES AND RISKS

These days, you can be your own boss from the get-go with the emergence of the gig economy. You can also choose your own hours and work from anywhere, really. Think of the gig economy as side quests, and you pick up these quests (the gigs), which are individual jobs whenever you want. When you order food, the driver who brought your food is part of the gig economy.

Finding the Perfect Gig

With so many options, I am sure you can find something you enjoy in the gig economy. Many of the examples I've given can be considered freelance work, as well. You need to be smart about choosing your gigs and consider how they fit with school. Anything from pet sitting to online tutoring can be great, flexible options.

Also, one of the benefits is that you can test different things without having to commit to them for a long period.

Making Money Work for You

Managing your gig money is a little different from managing your part-time job money. This is mainly because you don't have a fixed salary coming in. Some weeks and months can be great, while others not so much. So managing your money is absolutely essential.

You should save during the good times so you can cover for when the quiet times come. Also, taxes aren't automatically taken out of your gig work, so when the time comes, you might want to have money saved to pay your taxes.

Challenges of the Gig Economy

If you want to succeed in this industry, it's all about building your reputation and relationships. You have to do great work, communicate clearly with customers, and be reliable. If you do that, you will have regular customers who will specifically request you.

BASICS OF ENTREPRENEURSHIP FOR TEENS

There are many teens who start businesses. To give you a few examples, Mark Zuckerberg launched Facebook from his dorm room (Ward, 2017). Palmer Luckey built the first Oculus VR prototype when he was just 16 (Startup Archive, 2024). Now, I'm not saying that you will launch a billion-dollar company (you might), but these are the most successful examples; there are many other moderately successful ones.

The Entrepreneur Within You

Being an entrepreneur is not about fancy suits or extremely complicated business plans (although having one is good). It's all about seeing the opportunities where others can't. Today, you have an advantage that adult entrepreneurs don't: time and being more in touch with what your peers need.

You know what's trending before it hits mainstream; this is huge. You can capitalize on that. It could be anything you think there should be a solution for. Just start thinking about what drives you crazy or what problems you notice.

Starting Small but Thinking Big

As I've said, you don't need to create Facebook. You can start with something simple that solves a real problem in your community. Maybe there are many people in your neighborhood who struggle with technology—that's an opening. You can start a tech support service, for instance. Again, go back to the drawing board and think about your skills and what you can offer.

Your Game Plan for Success

A business plan sounds very "adult," right? But you don't necessarily need an elaborate one. It's important that you have a map to know where you are and where you are going with your business. You can start with some basic questions and try to answer them: Who needs what you are offering? How much will they pay for it? What makes your idea different from others?

From there, you can start detailing what you want to do with your business, and things begin to make sense.

Finding Your Team

While you might be an entrepreneur, you don't have to do it all alone. In fact, you shouldn't because everyone needs help once in a while. You will need advisors or mentors. Essentially, people who have lived in a similar situation can give you their experience so you don't have to fall for the same mistakes.

These people might already be around you in local business groups. If not, you can find online communities. You can join entrepreneurship forums or Facebook groups. There's plenty to explore.

One thing you should always keep in mind—especially in the beginning—is that starting a business and turning it successful takes time. You will make mistakes (everyone does), and some of your ideas won't work out. However, that's totally fine; that's part of the process. What's important is that you learn from these mistakes and adapt.

FINANCIAL PLANNING FOR YOUNG ENTREPRENEURS

Alright, so you've got your business up and running (well done, you!). Maybe you are already seeing some money coming in, which is great. But making money is only a part of it; there's more.

Yes, I'm talking about financial planning. Again, it is a strategy just like you would use in a video game. Perhaps your immediate goal to make enough money to buy new equipment or materials, and that's fine. That's your short-term mission. But what about the long term? Think about that.

For illustration purposes, let's say you are running a tech support business, and your short-term goal is to earn enough money to get better tools. Then, the medium-term could be to create a business website to bring in more clients. The long-term goal would be to open a real computer repair shop or launch your own app. Whatever your goal is, this is the process you have to follow—be sure to always have each goal in mind.

Your Business Budget

Budgeting is another one of those words that we wince when we hear them. I totally get that, but it's not as complicated as you might imagine. A budget lets you know what's coming in and out of your business money-wise. Again, start simple; you don't need an extremely complicated budget as of now. Just grab a notebook or your phone and open the Notes app. Then, write down everything you spend money on for your business. These are your expenses—anything from supplies to equipment.

Then, look at what comes in and track every single dollar you earn. There might be patterns, such as different services you provide, that bring in more money. Or look at which clients come back regularly. These things are important to know so you know what to continue marketing and where you can improve your business.

Reinvesting in Your Business

When you start making money with your business, you shouldn't just start spending it. While saving is an option, you might want to reinvest that money into your business so you can make more money. You need to invest some experience points in leveling up a character in a game instead of spending everything on armor. This is exactly the same. You might need better equipment so you can improve your services or spend more on marketing to bring in more clients.

Handling Financial Challenges

Now, there's something that you need to know. Sometimes (quite often, actually), businesses face tough times. Your favorite streamers probably have had months without any views or even where their viewership dropped; this is part of the game. You shouldn't try to avoid this. Instead, take it as an opportunity to understand what you can do better and prepare.

Emergency funds are important not only for your personal finances but also for your business. Always keep some money saved for when things turn sour. Your laptop might crash, your printer might break—anything can happen. However, having setbacks is temporary and is not a business-ending disaster.

There are also seasonal changes that you might need to account for. If you have a lawn care business, winters can be a little rough, or if you have a tutoring service, summers might be a little slower. You have to plan for these periods by saving extra during busy times.

7

ADVANCED MONEY MANAGEMENT

N ow, you've got the basics of money management and a little more, but managing your money is continuous learning, which we will explore in this chapter. As a teen, you are getting closer to some major life changes—this is both exciting and a little overwhelming. Maybe you're eyeing your first car, preparing for college, getting your first part-time job, or close to moving out from your parents (to go to college). These are big life changes, and you have to make decisions that can impact your life in the next few years. And this is why you need some more advanced money management skills.

In this chapter, we will be looking at all of that. I'm not going to lie; some of the things we might talk about might seem a little intimidating (but, really, they aren't). Negotiation skills, planning for big purchases, and even starting to think about retirement (yes, I know it's early, but the sooner, the better).

Let's break down these concepts so you can better understand them and not feel bored. Trust me, you won't.

NEGOTIATION SKILLS: GETTING THE BEST DEAL

How often do you hear the sentence, "That's the price; take it or leave?" And how many times have you just accepted that? Quite often, if not always, right? Most prices are not set in stone. That car you want has a negotiable price. Your first salary at your part-time job? Absolutely negotiable. What you need to know is how to negotiate these in your favor.

More Than Just Haggling

Negotiation has nothing to do with being aggressive. Movies are often inaccurate when it comes to these things. It's not always smooth-talking, and then you get the deal. Real negotiation is a dance where both parties work together to find a solution that works for everyone involved.

We have examples of negotiations all around us; for instance, when you and your friend are trying to decide what movie to watch. Maybe you want an action movie, and your friend wants a comedy. You don't yell at one another (if you do, let me tell you, there are better ways to decide) until one gives up. You have to be prepared for any type of negotiation. There are three main things you want to think about beforehand: What you want, what you are willing to accept, and when you should walk away. Say you are about to buy your first car, and your ideal price is $5000, but you're willing to go up to $6000, but anything above that number is a deal-breaker. These are your target, walkaway, and resistance points.

Real Situations, Real Negotiations

Besides deciding what movie to watch with your friend, I'm sure you've come across other situations that felt more like a negotiation. For instance, maybe you negotiated with your parents about extending your curfew. Let's use the example of purchasing your first car again.

The dealer says $8000, but you've done your research (you always have to do your research. Always!) and know a similar car is selling for $6000. You shouldn't just accept the price the dealer gave you or just walk away. You can negotiate (in fact, you *should* negotiate). Show them the research you've done, point out any issues with the car, and make a reasonable counteroffer.

The Power Moves of Pro Negotiators

All the pro negotiators have tricks up their sleeves (that's why they are pros), and I'm going to teach you some of them. Silence. Not you. I mean, let the silence work in your favor. Just sit there quietly and let the other party fill the silence. It's amazing how often they will offer you a better deal just to break the silence.

Another great strategy is the "if-then" strategy, and it is a favorite of mine. Instead of just asking for something, offer something in return. For example, you could say, "If I can pay cash today, would you consider lowering the price?" More often than not, the other party will agree or at least be willing to negotiate in your favor.

One more tip: You should always start with a reasonable offer. So, if you're selling something and want $50, don't ask for $150—unless you're prepared for a hard no. Instead, aim for $60 or $70 to give yourself room to negotiate without overpricing from the start. Negotiation is about finding a balance that works for both parties.

Practice Makes Perfect

It's normal to feel nervous when you're about to enter a negotia-tion; even adults feel that way. But practicing, like everything else, can really help. You should begin with smaller negotiations like the thrift shop or the flea market. Alternatively, you can make up scenarios to build your skills.

To give you a few examples, you can start with a scenario where you're buying a phone from a classmate or asking for a better price on a slightly damaged item at the store. You can always negotiate with your parents about allowances or chores. The more you practice, the more natural it will feel to you.

ADVANCED BUDGETING: PLANNING FOR BIG PURCHASES

We've already talked about goals and how to set them. Here, I'm going to talk about how to budget and plan for big purchases because we all will need to at some point.

Getting Real With the Numbers

Grab your phone or notebook and write down that big purchase you want. How much does it actually cost? Do your research; don't just guess it. You need accurate numbers. Many websites will help you compare prices on everything from cars to computers and anything else you can think of. If you're planning a trip, check hotels, ticket costs, and anything else you might need for that trip. Get accurate numbers.

Breaking Down Your Savings Goals

Now, it's time to strategize. Say that the iPhone you want is $1000. If you want it in 6 months, you need to save $167 a month. If this still sounds a little overwhelming, then try $42 a week or even $6 a day. Less scary, right? Doesn't it sound more tangible?

Making Room in Your Budget

There's a common mistake among teens: They get so excited about savings that they forget about their regular expenses. You still need money, after all, either for your coffee runs or outings with friends. This is the part where you have to be great at juggling everything. Take a look at your current spending and check where you can cut costs. Maybe go to Starbucks less often and have coffee at home instead.

Boosting Your Savings Game

You can look for ways to boost your income while saving: pick up a few extra shifts at your part-time job, start a side hustle, or offer help to your neighbors with yard work. Every single extra dollar is welcome and helps you reach your goal faster.

Another way to boost your savings is to use tech (in most cases, apps). Mint, which we talked about before, is great for tracking your progress, as is EveryDollar. Also, they are free to use and can help you track your progress really easily.

LONG-TERM SAVINGS STRATEGIES

When it comes to long-term savings, there's a massive difference between saving for those Air Jordans you want next month (short-term) and saving for the "future" you who's going to need actual adult stuff (long-term).

Why Should You Care About Retirement?

Retirement is far away; I know that. After all, you haven't even started college. But if you start saving now, you can save some serious money. Remember compound interest? That's why your savings can blow up. If you start saving $50 a month at the age of 16, by the time you retire (at 65), you could have over $175,000 (assuming a 7% return). Don't wait until you're in your 20s or 30s; you'll be losing quite some money if you do.

Getting Started With Your First Retirement Account

You can start a retirement account called a Roth IRA as soon as you start earning some income (even through your part-time). With this type of account, any money you put in grows tax-free. There are other types of retirement accounts, but this is the basic one.

So, how do you get one? Since you're under 18 (maybe), you will need a custodial Roth IRA, which your parents or guardian need to help you open. Companies like Charles Schwab or Fidelity offer such accounts with zero fees, and you can start with only $1. All you need is some earned income (and this has to be money you actually earn from your part-time, for instance, not your grand-ma's gifts) and, as I've said, an adult to help you set it up and open it. The process is straightforward:

- Choose a company (Fidelity, Charles Schwab, or Vanguard are solid choices).
- Have your parents or guardians open the custodial account online.
- Link a bank account to transfer money.
- Start investing.

As of today (2024), you can put up to $7,000 into your Roth IRA every year, but obviously, you put what you can into it (Sham, 2024).

Picking the Right Place to Put Your Money

Different goals need different strategies. For instance, you might want a high-yield savings account or a 529 plan (which is specifically for education) for your college fund. When it comes to your Roth IRA, you can invest in something more aggressive since you won't need the money until you retire.

Adjusting Your Plans

Life is not as predictable as you might think, and sometimes we need to change our plans. This happens to all of us. Maybe you prefer to start a business instead of going to college, or you prefer to focus on saving for an apartment instead of your dream car. When this happens, you need to review your goals (actually, you should review your goals every few months, even if nothing changes). Your financial goals should always match your life goals.

LEGAL AND FINANCIAL RESPONSIBILITIES AS YOU TURN 18

So, if you're not 18 years old already, you will soon be. And once you are, you will legally be an adult. Simply put, you're about to enter a world where your signatures actually count for something.

Up until now, your parents had to sign for everything, but those days are over. Now, your signature carries real weight. If you want a new phone plan, you can sign it yourself. The same is true for a lot of things, such as car loans and lease agreements for your new apartment. Whenever you sign something, you are legally hooked on whatever you agreed on, so read the small print!

Money Moves That Matter Now

Now, your relationship with money is more serious than ever. The direct deposits from your job might be getting bigger if you become a full-time employee, but with that, there are also other responsibilities. You are not just saving for clothes; now, you're saving to rent an apartment and to pay for utilities. Netflix or Amazon Prime subscriptions are probably the smallest bill you will pay. Car insurance is a whole other beast now that you pay it, and keeping the lights on actually costs money! So, yes, you have to start thinking about all of these things.

Besides money, there are other things that are more important now too. I'm talking about legal documents. You have to keep your driver's license and state ID updated, among other things. You should also start getting organized when it comes to documents because you don't know when you're going to need them. So having them in one place, or at least a place you know where they are, is very useful. Health insurance and medical decisions are all on you too. If you're heading to college or just moving out, you might want to consider a medical directive, which is a document saying who can make decisions for you if something happens. I know we don't like to talk about this stuff, but it's very important. Just start thinking about these things now so you have it all figured out when you turn 18.

The Credit Card Talk and Financial Pitfalls

Credit card companies are going to come at you as if you are a celebrity once you turn 18. There will be "amazing" offers in your mailbox. If you decide to get a credit card, which we've seen can be good, start with a basic one just to build credit. Only use it for small, regular purchases you know you can pay back right away.

Your best friend wants you to co-sign their car loan? Probably not the best idea, trust me. Even if they say they will make every single payment, you're the one who has to pay if they can't, and you know how unpredictable life is. When it comes to apartment leases, read everything (like *everything*).

PLANNING FOR COLLEGE AND MANAGING STUDENT LOANS

It's now time to talk about the "elephant in the room": college expenses. We all know college can be really expensive, and you are probably aware of the rough numbers. Maybe a $40,000 or $50,000 price on your dream college seems dire, but almost no one pays for it in full.

Finding Free Money

Before we get into loans, there's money to be "earned" that you don't need to pay back. Scholarship applications are the way to go.

There are scholarships for everything. The FAFSA (Free Application for Federal Student Aid) is what you should check because it's your chance to get grants (which are essentially free government money), work-study jobs (campus jobs that work around your class schedule), and federal loans. You should fill them out as soon as possible to get a faster response and assess your options.

The Student Loan

Chances are you may need a student loan. They're not necessarily the enemy, but they are not free money like grants. Federal loans should be the first thing you check because they come with perks such as income-based repayment plans and forgiveness options. Private loans, if possible, should be avoided.

The issue with loans is that if you borrow $40,000, they quickly turn into $50,000 by the time you have to start paying it back (yes, it is also thanks to compound interest, which does not always work in our favor). Use a loan calculator before you sign up for any loan to see the type of monthly payments you have to make after you graduate.

Life on a College Budget

Life on a college budget might stink, but I guarantee you those are some of the best days of your life. Now, textbooks can cost more than your phone, but here's a tip: You can rent them out or buy used ones. And there's a plethora of random college fees that you will have to live with.

A budget is your best tool here. It accounts for wants and needs (and you definitely need textbooks). You need to eat, but you don't have to order DoorDash every two days. Start tracking spending now before you go to college to have a better idea.

The Post-Graduation Game Plan

Let's fast-forward to graduation. The loans you took out are here, and they are real! But you have options. For instance, federal loans come with different repayment plans. There are forgiveness programs if you work in public service or in certain fields. And they can also be based on your income.

Just have a plan before bills start coming in. This can be done during your senior year when you can begin to map out your post-graduation budget. You can include expected loan payments, rent, car payments, and all that adult stuff. It might not be easy, but with planning, you can definitely do it!

8

FINANCIAL TECHNOLOGY AND TOOLS

I t's probably hard for you to imagine a world without apps or smartphones. And as you know, money didn't miss the party; it turned digital too. Paper checks are a thing of the past if you even know what they are. This is perhaps the chapter that's going to feel more natural to you, and it's all about managing digital money. I mean, you already use Venmo to split the cost of the food you and your friends spend on DoorDash, and I'm sure you are familiar with Apple and Google Pay. However, there's so much more than that, and you might not be aware of everything.

We will be looking at all the different ways you can make money management easier. We will be looking at apps that turn your phone into an extremely powerful money management tool. But, with all of this technology, quite a bit of responsibility comes with it. Yes, these money management apps are more efficient, faster, and convenient, but everything has challenges, and this is no exception.

MUST-HAVE FINANCIAL APPS FOR TEENS

In the way we have different social media apps for different things, such as ways of interacting with content or communicating with friends, there are also multiple money management apps, and you should be aware of some of them so you can better pick which ones are best for you.

Your Financial App Arsenal

Beginning with budgeting apps, PocketGuard is one of the best out there. It can connect to your bank account and categorize your expenses automatically so you always know exactly how much money you're spending. Greenlight, for instance, is specifically designed for teens and is extremely accessible. When it comes to saving money, Acorns is fantastic; working as a digital piggy bank, it can round up your change on purchases and add it to your savings or investments.

There are many others that are worth checking, such as Goodbudget, GoHenry, BusyKid, or YNAB.

Feature You Should Look Out For

An app can look really fancy, but if it's not helping you achieve your goals, it's as good as nothing. The great apps have some good features that are worth using. For instance, real-time tracking is great so you know exactly how much and where you are spending your money, as well as how much you have in savings or within your budget right now. Customizable budgeting categories are also a useful feature because we are all different and have different needs. Maybe you spend more on gaming than clothes, so your app should let you set up categories that actually match your real life.

Push notifications are a must (and thankfully, most good apps have them). They are great for keeping you aware of what you're spending and oftentimes prevent you from making bad decisions.

How These Apps Change How You Handle Money

Many of us have tried to keep an accurate record of our spending on the Notes app, but it's hard and time-consuming. All of the apps mentioned above work for you in this regard. They keep accurate records of everything, and you don't even have to do anything.

If you're trying to save up to see a band you like, these apps can show you exactly how close you are to your goal, and some can even suggest ways to get there faster simply by analyzing your spending and where you can cut back.

Let me give you a real-life example. Anna is a typical 17-year-old, and she started using Step when she got her first job in the local coffee shop. She had absolutely no idea where her money was going until she started using the app. Because of it, she realized she was spending almost $50 only on snacks at school. She cut that in half and put the difference toward a laptop she wanted to buy.

ONLINE BANKING: A STEP-BY-STEP GUIDE

Since you're managing your money from your phone, it's imperative that you know how to use the banking app from your bank. You can't manage your money if you don't know the ins and outs of your main money management app. Most major banks have banking apps; I'm talking about Bank of America, Chase, or Capital One, and all of them have super easy-to-use apps, but local banks can also have great apps.

Once you have your bank account set up, you will probably receive an email from the bank to set up your online banking app. This should be straightforward; you'll just need to create a username and password.

Great Features You Can Actually Use

I've mentioned this feature before, but I'm not getting tired of emphasizing it. That birthday check your grandma gave you can be deposited with the snap of a picture! A few days later, you have the money in your account (yes, it is often not instant, but at least you don't have to go down to the bank).

You can send (and receive) money instantly through the app, as well as set up automatic payments for all the subscriptions you have, so you don't get that "payment denied" message ever again! Most banking apps nowadays can do a lot more. While you might not need it right away, you can open a credit card account, check your credit score, or check if you can be approved for a loan or a mortgage.

Why Online Banking Is Perfect for Busy Teens

Well, perhaps the best feature of online banking is that you can manage your money 24/7 without having to wait for the bank to open on a Monday morning. Too busy to get down to the bank? That's not a problem. Want to see if your part-time wage hit your account? You can do it in seconds. Also, most online banking apps give you detailed spending so you know where all your money is going with graphs and charts, and all of that.

To make the most out of your online banking app, I suggest you turn on your notifications so you know when money is coming in or out of your account or if there are upcoming payments. Use the budgeting tools they offer; while they might not be as sophisticated as dedicated budgeting apps, sometimes they're all you need.

Staying Safe and Smart Online

Please make it a habit to check your account at least once or twice a week. You can look for strange charges you are not aware of or don't recognize (because, you know, fraud). Most banking apps let you dispute charges right from the app. You should also keep an eye on your account balance before making big purchases because sometimes the app might say you have $200, but if you made a purchase right before, it might take some time for you to see the change. Avoid public Wi-Fi when you're using your banking app; you never know who could be lurking and getting access to your information.

UNDERSTANDING AND USING MOBILE PAYMENTS

Mobile payments are one of the greatest features of mobile banking and other apps that allow you to do that. Essentially, you can pay for stuff just by tapping your phone or smartwatch. If you have an iPhone, you can use Apple Pay; if you have an Android, you can use Google Pay; and if you have a Samsung Galaxy phone, you can use Samsung Pay (I know, they are not very original with their names, but they are efficient). It's just like having a wallet on your smartwatch or phone. Simple and easy.

Getting Your Mobile Payments Set Up

This is actually pretty easy to do. On an iPhone, Apple Pay is already installed, and all you have to do is pen your Wallet app and add the card (often, you can just take a front and back picture of your card). For Android users, head to Google Pay (or Samsung Pay if you have a Galaxy) and follow the instructions.

When setting up your card on your phone, your bank might send you a message with a code to verify it's really you (this is completely normal!). Once you've done that, you can set up a pass-code or use the fingerprint/face ID for an extra layer of security.

Keeping Your Mobile Payments Secure

You should try to avoid any mobile payment issues. To do this, the first thing you should do is lock down your phone using string pass-words and definitely use the face ID or fingerprint feature. Never ever share your passwords or payment information with anyone. Use only your phone's official app store to download payment apps and nothing else. I know you know this, but avoid public Wi-Fi!

One last thing about mobile payments: Just because it's super easy to pay for things doesn't mean you should go on a spending spree. While these apps make it easy to just tap for things and get them, it is still money you're spending, and it's fairly easy to lose track of it. Put some limits on yourself at all times.

STAYING SAFE WITH ONLINE TRANSACTIONS

The internet can be quite a sketchy place. I'm sure you're aware of this. This is especially true about money. Who sells designer Jordans at 90% off? Sketchy, right? What about those random DMs saying you can make quick cash? Sketchy. Unfortunately, scammers are getting pretty good these days, and it's getting increasingly harder to spot what is a scam and what isn't. But there are some things you can pay attention to that can save you from falling into these scams.

Keeping Your Digital Life Secure

Thankfully, cybersecurity has been evolving too. Regarding this, there are some basic things you should do. For instance, when buying something from a shopping website, always look for the little padlock symbol next to the website's address and make sure the URL starts with "https://." When you create accounts, don't use the same password you use everywhere. You can use one password but add in some numbers and other symbols to make it harder to figure out.

Keeping your apps updated is very important because those updates are usually fixes that the app company made because they found out scammers are using loopholes to get information from people.

Protecting Your Personal Info

I think this goes without saying (even though I have mentioned it before): don't give away your personal info to every website you create an account for. It's like giving your house keys to strangers. For an extra layer of protection, consider using a VPN (Virtual Private Network) when you're shopping or using online banking. This gives you an "invisible shield," placing your IP address in another place. There are free VPNs, and some of the paid ones have student discounts, so make the best of it.

When There's a Breach

Sometimes, not even the most cautious person is immune to security breaches. This often comes in the form of weird transactions from your card. If this happens, contact your bank right away; most of them have 24/7 fraud hotlines, and the faster you report, the better it is when it comes to your protection. Change your passwords immediately, just in case.

Take screenshots of all suspicious activity, and if you got scammed from social media, you can report the account that scammed you. This is important so other people don't fall for the same scammer.

You should also report online scams to the FTC (Federal Trade Commission) directly through their website. This is because they take this very seriously, especially when it involves teens. And there's a better chance of actually catching the bad guys.

Please remember that getting scammed doesn't mean you're stupid or anything. As I've said, scammers are getting increasingly better at scamming. What's important is to understand what went wrong and be more careful next time.

THE FUTURE OF MONEY: WHAT LIES AHEAD

Now let's talk about something that will definitely make you wonder what we can achieve: the future of money. You already know that the way we use money is changing. Physical cash is more of a rarity nowadays with everything in the palm of your hand.

What's Hot in the Money World

For one, digital banking is already here and becoming the new normal. More and more people are changing the classic physical banks and turning to digital banks. Ally Bank or Starling Bank are just some of the options. Essentially, these banks don't have physical locations, so you can't go down to the bank branch if you need something. Everything is online. This allows these types of banks to save money on renting physical spaces and get more benefits for their customers. Plus, all of their banking apps are top-notch because, you know, it's the only way to interact with the bank itself. Also, the reputed ones are 100% safe and have protections in place just like your typical bank.

And, of course, there's crypto. As you know, crypto is quite volatile at the moment, but it is certainly something that will continue to improve, and chances are more people will begin using it more and more. It's super secure with their digital ledger, which perhaps can even be implemented in our fiat money. What's even cooler is that many countries are already mostly cashless. Sweden and China are places where cash is becoming increasingly rare. Every transaction happens through smartphones and smartwatches or even facial recognition. I know, right? You just leave the store, and money is taken out of your account. You don't need to checkout. There are already some stores around the world (mainly owned by Amazon, of course) where this can be done.

Tech That's Changing the Game

Besides the above, other technology is emerging and promises to change the financial world completely (and many other industries). Artificial intelligence (AI) is no longer a sci-fi dream; it is happening right now (and extremely fast). You can have a financial advisor in your pocket 24/7, and they can help you make better financial decisions about investing or saving. Everything is based on your own situation.

Biometrics is another interesting technology, and fingerprint scanning on your phone is just the beginning. Actually, we already pay for things with facial recognition on our phones, so there's that. But maybe in the future, we can use our voices, or who knows what else? A few banks are already experiencing voice recognition for security, which will make it even harder to hack into accounts.

Getting Ready for the Future of Money

So, how do you prepare for this crazy but amazing world? The first bit of advice I have is to stay curious and learn as much as you can. Don't wait for things to happen; read and experience new technology, and stay ahead of the game. Follow tech news and pay attention to financial apps and the different services they roll out. The more you know, the better prepared you will be.

Keep in mind that just because it's a new technology and maybe it's trending, it doesn't mean it's 100% safe. You have to do your research beforehand and understand who produces that technology and what precautions they have implemented.

Speculative Technology

Now, what I'm about to talk about here is not certain. There are technologies being developed, for sure, but that doesn't mean they will ever be rolled out into the mainstream public. It could very well happen.

One of these technologies is a universal digital currency, which essentially is a currency that works everywhere in the world. So, there would be no need to exchange between currencies, and often lose money while doing it. There are also smart contracts (now this is real and often used in a cryptocurrency called Ethereum), which automatically handle things like allowances or part-time job payments.

Another technology is virtual reality banking, which comes full circle. We had physical branches; now we have online banks, and maybe we will have the chance to go down to the bank without leaving our room by "walking" into a virtual reality bank and actually talking to another person to help us out. Micropayments might be something that can happen where you can pay tiny amounts (such as cents) for things like reading an article online or listening to a song.

These are just some things that we might be able to do quite soon if everything aligns properly. However, I'm sure there will be things we can't even imagine that will occur, and that's where the fun is, really.

9

BUILDING WEALTH

S ometimes, we need to wait to get the thing we want. You might need to save for a few months and be diligent before spending money, but if you start building your wealth as a teenager, you can get the things you want more easily. Wealth building sounds like something only adults do, but we've seen throughout the book that it's not true. You can start right now. And we've also seen that you don't need tons of money to get started.

Look at it this way: You know those amazing professional athletes? They weren't just born great; they started working on their skills at a very early age. They learned the techniques and the strategies, and now what they do looks easy. Building wealth is not that different. If you start learning and practicing smart money moves now, it will get a lot easier later on, and you will be building wealth from a young age (you know, compound interest and all).

So, we will be looking at how you can build wealth in a way that makes sense to you now. We'll cover things like starting to invest, why you should join investment clubs, and how adults can be mentors when it comes to guiding you on your wealth-building path.

This is not all about making money; it is more like giving you choices later in life. If you want to travel after high school, you can, or if you want to start your own YouTube channel, you can do that too. Anyway, let's get to it.

The Concept of Financial Independence

Not having to ask your parents for money is a great start, but I want you to think bigger. What if you never had to work a job you don't like just to pay your bills? This is real financial independence. It's not about being filthy rich but more like having enough money coming in from your investments and other sources that you can cover all your expenses without depending on your regular paycheck.

Right now, you might need to work a weekend job to buy the things you want, but when you're financially independent, your money will be working for you instead of the other way around. You get to choose how you want to spend your time instead of having to work a job you don't like.

How to Get There?

Well, you will need strategy, patience, and the right moves at the right time, but it has nothing to do with being lucky or an absolute mad genius, mind you. Building financial independence takes consistent effort and smart decision-making. Here are the main ways it happens for most people:

Aggressive saving is one path to financial independence. You don't need to eat ramen noodles every day—it's about being smart and saving large amounts of money whenever you can. Cutting out unnecessary expenses and automating your savings can make this process easier. For example, maybe you can put 50% of your income into savings. That might sound challenging at first, but starting small and building the habit over time can make a big difference.

Investing wisely is one of the best ways to grow your wealth. Don't let your money sit in a savings account, earning little to no interest. Instead, invest in stocks, bonds, and index funds to make your money grow faster. Compound interest works wonders over time, and with consistent investments, you can build a strong financial foundation. Just remember to do your research or speak with a financial advisor before diving into the market.

Another way to build financial independence is through passive income—money that comes in whether you're working or not. This could be from a YouTube channel that generates ongoing revenue, a small business that runs itself, or a rental property where you earn income from tenants. The key is to invest time and effort upfront so that these income streams continue to flow with minimal active involvement in the future.

The Math Behind Financial Freedom

So, how much do you actually need to be financially independent? While this is hard to pinpoint, there's this 4% rule that financial experts like to use (Kagan, 2024). Essentially, the rule says you take your yearly expenses and multiply them by 25, and that's roughly how much you need to save up. Let's look at an example.

Say you'll need $40,000 a year to live comfortably, which is about $3,333 a month. Now, multiply this by 25, and you'd need about $1 million invested to be financially independent. It might sound like a lot, but that's why starting young is great. If you start by the age of 18 and earn an average of 7% return a year, you just need to invest $450 a month to hit $1 million by the age of 45.

Living Smart to Get There Faster

The choices you make in life can speed up the process of financial independence. It has nothing to do with being cheap but about being smart with your money and knowing exactly what makes you happy. If we consider minimalism, some teens are finding having fewer, better-quality things actually makes them happier than having a lot of things they never use. So, instead of buying every new game that comes out, choose your favorite series and buy them instead. When it comes to fashion, have a smaller wardrobe of clothes that lasts longer rather than a lot of clothes that you have to throw away every month because they are cheap quality.

Susan, a 16-year-old from California, began tracking every single dollar she spent using PocketGuard. She soon realized she was spending over $100 on bus rides to get to school when she could have ridden her bike for 15 minutes instead. So, she started riding to school and only got the bus when it was raining. She was able to save up almost $100 a month. She started putting that money in her savings account, and in a year, she had about $1,000. If she starts putting that money toward investments, at a yearly return of 7%, she could have over $7,000 over the next 5 years.

WEALTH BUILDING: IT'S NOT JUST FOR ADULTS

Okay, let's bust a myth right now: You don't need to wait until you get a "real" job to start building your wealth. As you know, compound interest helps those who start early, and you can do it with your allowance or part-time job.

Tools Making Investments Possible for You

You already know you can get a custodial account when you start investing. But we haven't gotten too deep into this yet. There are two main ones: the Uniform Gift to Minors Act (UGMA) and the Uniform Transfer to Minors Act (UTMA) accounts. These allow you to invest in stocks, bonds, and mutual funds before you turn 18.

Besides that, there are all the apps we talked about before, such as Greenlight or BusyKid, that help you learn about investing while you are actually doing it. Some of these even help you buy fractional shares (which are little parts of a share at a smaller cost), so you can get expensive stocks like Google or Amazon for way less.

And there are, of course, savings accounts designed for teens. You won't be making as much interest, but it's good to diversify your money.

Developing Your Wealth Mindset

This is a very, very important part of the whole process and a part that most people tend to overlook. Building your wealth mindset is as much about money as it is about the way you think about money. You have to think about the long term when everyone around you seems to be thinking about what's going to happen tomorrow. Your friends might be spending their entire allowance or paycheck on clothes and games; you're thinking about how you can grow your money.

You can still have fun and buy things you want and enjoy, but once again, it's about making smart choices. Another big part of the wealth mindset is patience. And I know many teenagers lack this. You're growing a garden, and these things take time. You need consistent effort and the ability to wait for results. Once it starts growing, you will understand that it was worth the wait.

Real-Life Stories

Mike began to resell sneakers online at the age of 15. Instead of spending all of his profit on more sneakers, he invests about 70% of what he makes into index funds. Two years later, his investment account had grown to over $15,000 (Ctanujit Classes, n.d.). Jessica is another teen who was able to shift to a money mindset. She used her coding skills to build websites for local businesses. She put half of her earnings into a custodial account, investing in tech stocks. By the age of 18, she had built a portfolio worth $20,000.

What do you think is the common thread here? Neither of them came from a wealthy family. They had a plan, they were patient, and they understood that starting early gave them a massive advantage.

INVESTMENT CLUBS AND GROUPS: LEARNING TOGETHER

Perhaps in school, you've joined a study group to tackle a hard subject. If so, investment groups sort of work in a similar way. But instead of learning for a test, you are learning how to grow your money with other like-minded people. Just like any other group, you can meet regularly face-to-face or online and maybe even pool your money together as an investment group.

Making Your Club Work

If you're starting a club instead of joining one, it's not that hard. You first need to find some friends who are interested in learning about investment. Ideally, anything between 5 and 10 people is enough. You want a minimum amount so you can have good discussions but not so many that not everyone can chime in or voice their opinions without getting too confusing and loud.

To get started, you can:

- pick a regular meeting time.
- choose a cool name (not entirely necessary, but why wouldn't you?).

- get a teacher or an adult who knows investing to help.
- set some basic rules (such as minimum contribution requirements).

If you plan pool your money and invest together (which, by the way, is not a requirement), you will certainly need an adult to help.

Learning the Smart Way

So, the best part of these clubs is that you don't need to try and figure out everything alone. You're both teaching and learning from others. Maybe one of the members of your club is really into research, while others are great at crypto. You can divide up tasks to make them more interesting.

When it comes to activities, you can have a "stock pitch" session where every member presents an investment idea, or you can create a mock portfolio to practice investing without the risk of losing real money. Other activities, such as inviting successful investors to talk to you or tracking and discussing real-world financial news, can really affect your investments in a positive way.

Case Studies

The "Future Investors of Wilson High" is a group where five friends got together in their school library during lunch breaks. Each member picked a different sector to research, such as tech, retail, renewable energy, etc. Then, they used a stock market simulator app to practice trading and kept a shared spreadsheet of their research. After about six months or so, their group had grown to 10 and caught their economics teacher's attention. He helped them set up a real investment account where each member contributed

$15 monthly. So, in their first month, they split the pooled money between the S&P 500 index fund and shares in companies that they used on a daily basis, such as Amazon, Apple, Nike, etc.

But two years later, and this is where it gets really interesting, all of them had improved their grades in both economics and math. Three members started money-related YouTube channels, and one even got a part-time job at a local investment company. And, of course, they all made money from those investments and became great investors later on.

READING FINANCIAL NEWS: WHY IT MATTERS FOR TEENS

If you're not into reading financial news, you will be missing a lot of important information. If you just listen to or see TV news when your parents have it at dinner time, maybe you will get one or two financial news stories. As an investor, you have to be more into financial news and read as much as you can, so you can make better investment choices.

Understanding What's Behind the Headlines

For example, when Apple launches a new iPhone, you shouldn't just care about the cool new feature the new iPhone might have. That launch affects Apple's stock price, and it could impact your investments if you own any Apple shares. If you're saving up for college, headlines about student loan rates or changes in college tuition can also directly affect you and how much you will need to save. Or maybe you have heard something about the new minimum wage, which, if you have a part-time job, means you might be getting more money, but it also means that some stores at the mall might not be able to support such costs and might have to

close. So, don't just read the headlines; there's often a lot more
to it.

Don't Trust Everything You See

Not everything you read about money or finances is true. Maybe
you remember when everyone on social media said that cryptocurrency would make everyone rich. While some got richer,
many lost money. Again, you have to be smart about your money
and don't fall for everything you hear.

If you see a headline that says, "This Stock Will Make You Rich
Tomorrow," it's probably not true. As we've learned, these things
take time. Take a step back; you can still read it, but be mindful
that these headlines are mostly for clicks.

Where to Find Reliable Money News?

With all this said, where can you find trustworthy news that isn't just clickbait? Well, there are many great places you can start. Robinhood, the stock market app, has a great news section. Plain Bagel on YouTube is an excellent source of information about personal and investment news. Even Investopedia has pretty much everything related to money and investments.

Making the News Work for You

So, now, how do you act on the news you read to benefit you? If you read that Nike just opened a lot of new stores and they are having sales, this might be a good opportunity (after thorough research, of course). Or maybe you read that interest rates are going up. This means that your savings account interest will go up, making you more money. But it also means that your car loan interest might be going up as well.

MENTORSHIP IN FINANCE: FINDING GUIDANCE

Even though what you're learning here seems pretty straightforward, it doesn't mean that sometimes, it isn't a little overwhelming. It can be, and I totally get that. That's why having someone with experience next to you can be really helpful. I'm talking about a mentor, someone who has gone through what you are going through and can guide you in the best direction.

It doesn't have to be someone with a degree in economics or anything. Just someone who has investments and knows how things work better than you do.

Finding Your Money Guide

Now, it's the part where you need to find someone who fits the description. And I always recommend first looking closer to home. Maybe you have an uncle or an aunt who started their own business. Or your friend's mom, who works in banking. Or even your school's math or economics teacher. Any of those would probably help you quite a lot. But maybe you don't have anyone around who can help you. In this case, your local library or community center might be the next best place. Also, many high schools have alumni networks with successful graduates who'd love to help current students.

Also, you can join a Discord server or a Reddit community about personal finance or investment. You should never share any personal info online, and you don't necessarily have to. Most of the time, these places have certified professionals you can ask questions.

Making the Relationship Work

Once you've found your mentor, you shouldn't just go to them and ask if they can be your mentor. It might be a little awkward. You can begin with specific questions about their experience, and it's important that you get to know them. And then, if and when they agree to be your mentor, you should always treat their time with respect. You should show up prepared for any meetings you might have. Write down questions you want to ask and share your progress. They will love to see you succeed.

10

BEYOND MONEY: FINANCIAL ETHICS AND RESPONSIBILITY

D o you sometimes come across your favorite influencer advertising for a cryptocurrency project just to find out later that the project is a scam? How about those "easy money" schemes going around that promise to double your earnings tomorrow? Just because there's a possibility of making money doing something doesn't mean you should. This is what people call financial ethics.

You might be scratching your head wondering where ethics come into the financial world, but they do, and they are quite important. It doesn't matter what the field is; having ethics is important because we all should try to be decent human beings. What if you find out that your best friend's side hustle is selling fake concert tickets? What would you do? What would be your ethical stance in that particular situation?

Here, we will be looking at financial ethics, which many books fail to address. We all live in one big shared world, so we need to be good to each other. Besides that, we will also be talking about sustainable investing because we should all care about our world while making money. We'll also cover how you can spot genuine investment opportunities and sketchy schemes.

THE ETHICS OF MONEY: MAKING MORALLY SOUND FINANCIAL DECISIONS

Okay, let's look at a hypothetical scenario: Say you are at the mall buying that jacket you've really wanted, and the cashier accidentally gives you $20 extra in change. No one else notices it. This should be easy money, right? Except that little voice in your head doesn't shut up. Well, that's having morals (if you actually go back and give the $20 back to the cashier). Financial ethics is all about making financial decisions that make you feel proud. If we look at this example, sure, free money sounds great, but what if someone did that to you? What if that cashier got in trouble for the missing $20, and they had it taken from their paycheck? That type of free money doesn't sound so good, right?

When you make ethical financial decisions, you're not just (hopefully) making money. You're also building a good reputation—a reputation that lets people know that you can be trusted.

Real-Life Money Dilemmas

Over your life, you will certainly come across some situations where you'll find a moral dilemma. For instance, you find a lost wallet at school. You could just take the cash and dump the wallet. But what if it was you? What if that student only had that money to eat for the rest of the day?

What if your friend starts a dropshipping business and asks you to write fake reviews for products you've never used? The money's not bad, but you'd be lying to people.

You could say that everyone does it. Alright, fine. But unethical money moves have a way of catching up with you sooner or later. Maybe that fake review will get you banned from the reviews platform. Or maybe there was a camera directly pointing at you when you found that student's wallet and a teacher saw you taking the money and dumping the wallet. Oh, the shame... and your reputation, of course.

What do you think happens to your favorite influencer when they get caught promoting scam products? Their reputation takes a massive hit.

Building Your Own Moral Compass

How can you figure out what's right when it comes to money? Here are some things I like to use:

- The Mirror Test: Could you look at yourself in the mirror and feel good about this decision?
- The Mom Test: Would you be comfortable telling your mom about what you did?
- The Public Test: If your decision was posted online, would you be okay with it?
- The Flip Test: What if someone did this to you?

Certain situations are not that clear, I know. But think about your actions before you actually do them.

SUPPORTING CHARITIES AND PHILANTHROPY AS A TEEN

It might not be as easy to help others when you don't have that much money yet, but the truth is that you don't have to have a lot of money to make a difference. For example, instead of spending $5 on Starbucks that day, you can provide school supplies for a kid who needs them.

What's Philanthropy All About?

While the word "philanthropy" sounds really fancy, it just means helping others. It's about making a difference by helping those who have real needs, just like you would help your little brother or sister get started in a video game (but on a much larger, more impactful scale).

Fortunately, we have philanthropy all around us, even though it often feels like it's never enough. You've probably seen a YouTuber who raises money for a cause. That's a perfect example of philanthropy in action. The key is to remember that it's not about the size of the donation or the big gestures; it's all about the intention behind the help and the act of giving.

Finding Your Cause

Now, we can't help everyone, but we can pick causes that are important to us and focus on them. Fortunately, people are different and choose different causes, so don't get hung up on not helping everyone. You want a cause that speaks to you. If you're passionate about climate change, there are ways to raise money for it. The same goes for mental health if, for instance, you have someone close to you who suffers. But there are so many other causes that you can join; I'm sure you will find your calling.

You still have to do your homework when it comes to causes you want to help, and this means research. You see, some organizations are really sketchy. Unfortunately, that also happens in an industry all about giving to others. So, researching organizations is very important. There are many out there that promise but never deliver. You can look at their website and try to find out where the money goes. You can also use a website called "Charity Navigator," which lets you check the ratings and donors of different organizations.

The best organizations are very clear about what they do, who they help, and where the donations go. They focus on transparency, so you can easily see how your contribution is making a difference. Most reputable organizations allocate the majority of their funds directly to helping people and supporting causes rather than spending large portions on administrative costs. They don't have huge salaries for the organizers or fancy offices. This is something to look out for when deciding where to donate.

Making an Impact Without Breaking the Bank

As I've said before, you can help without spending too much of your money. In fact, you often can offer more than just money. You can offer your time or skills; they might be just as valuable. To give you an example, your local pet shelter might need someone who is really good at photography; maybe that's you.

And there are many ways you can give back, depending on your skills. If you're into coding, you can help make a website for a charity. If you're good with music or have the necessary contacts, why don't you organize a benefit concert? Every ticket purchased is donated to the charity.

What's In It For You?

For you, there's probably a lot more than you first anticipated, and it goes beyond just feeling good about helping others, which is the best part. Being involved in philanthropy gives you real-life skills. You learn how to organize events, how to manage projects, or even how to solve different kinds of problems. You can add these to college applications because they are the types of skills your future college is looking for.

But, of course, it is so much more than resume building. When you help others, you connect with people who care about the same things as you. It's an excellent place to find mentors and make new friends.

Starting Your Giving Journey

As with everything we've seen, you should start small. Maybe you can skip a coffee run or two this month and donate that money to a cause you care about. Or maybe spend a weekend helping a local food bank. You see how it feels and talk to your friends about joining you, because everything is more fun with friends.

SUSTAINABLE INVESTING AND FINANCIAL CHOICES FOR A BETTER WORLD

There seems to be a wide movement to "save the earth" and fight climate change. Surely, you've heard of Greta Thunberg or many bands going green and sustainability everywhere you look, which is absolutely fantastic. But do you ever wonder how you can help? Well, in fact, you can help save the world with your money as an investor. It's all about the choices you make, really.

Making Money While Saving the Planet

Sustainable investment is investing in companies that are sustainable or that are doing good things to help the world. Say you are indecisive about two games (made by two different companies). One game is made by a company everyone knows is using unethical labor practices, and the second game is made by a company that gives some of its profits to charities. Sustainable investing is backing the good guys here.

Again, it's not all about feeling good; in investing, you still have to be smart about your money. Companies that care about the environment and care about their workers often do better in the long term because they think ahead. They are getting ready for the future, where clean energy is the way to go and workers' rights are absolutely important.

Where to Put Your Money?

Like any investment you make, research is the best way to find out. But to give you an idea, some companies are working on electric cars (not just Tesla, by the way), solar power, or coming up with better ways to recycle, while others are focused on making sure workers get fair pay and good working conditions. You should look at ESG funds, which stand for Environmental, Social, and Governance. These are mutual funds or index funds that focus on such companies, so it's a great way to start. Instead of just trying to pick individual stocks, you can get a bundle of sustainable companies to start with.

Your Daily Money Choices Matter Too

Of course, sustainable money is not just about investing. If you buy a reusable bottle instead of buying a plastic water bottle every time you're thirsty, that's a sustainable financial choice. Or choosing second-hand clothes instead of always buying brand new. Even the bank you pick can be a sustainable financial choice. This is because some banks invest in fossil fuels, for example, while others prefer to support the local community or invest in renewable energies.

Making It Work For You

You might have heard that sustainable stuff is more expensive, and the truth is that sometimes it is. Maybe the eco-friendly phone case you bought is worth twice as much as a regular one. Sustainable products tend to last longer, which saves you money in the long term. And, as I've said, sustainable companies tend to perform better over time.

Again, you don't have to go all in at once in your sustainable journey. You can start looking at where you spend your money now. Can you switch to a reusable coffee mug? Or just consider buying quality items that last longer instead of cheap ones that you will have to replace soon.

It's not about being perfect; it's about making better choices every day. Every sustainable decision you make with your money adds up to something bigger and better.

REVIEW REQUEST!!!!

Now that you've got all the tools to achieve financial independence, accumulate wealth, gain confidence in money management, and understand financial markets, it's time to pay it forward and help others do the same.

By sharing your honest opinion of this book on Amazon, you're not only letting other teenagers with limited financial literacy, understanding of investing principles, fear of making financial mistakes, or limited access to investment resources know where they can find the help they need, but you're also spreading the passion for investing among your peers.

Thank you for your contribution. The Teens community thrives when we share our knowledge and experiences, and you're playing a crucial role in keeping that momentum going.

Scan the QR code below to leave a review.

Keep shining bright, and let's continue empowering teenagers to take charge of their financial futures!

Your biggest fan,

Riley Wealth

CONCLUSION

Let's go back to when you started reading this book. It's likely that terms like compound interest or investment portfolios were completely foreign to you or gave you the shivers. What about now? Do you still feel the same way? No, those are just big words for quite simple concepts, really (adults just like to complicate things all the time). You can even participate in your parents' household budget meetings without feeling lost now. I want you to think about everything you've learned here for a second. We talked about budgeting and the many different ways you can approach it —and, by the way, I'm pretty sure you've mastered it or absolutely will once you get started. We also looked at compound interest and how your money can actually make you more money while you sleep. Or the "overwhelming" world of investing, which turned out not to be that scary after all. All you have to do is to start slowly.

Most importantly, you started your own path toward financial independence and becoming an adult who can follow your dreams without having money holding you back. Most people start thinking about money management and wealth building in their twenties or thirties, but you started now, and that's going to make a massive difference going forward. Within the investment side of things, we explored how you can avoid scams and how you can have your money help you while helping the planet and others.

Throughout this book, we've discussed how money is not just about getting rich. You have to make choices that align with your values and your goals. You can do this through sustainable investments, supporting ethical companies, or giving back to the community. While you are building wealth, you are also shaping the world around you for the benefit of everyone.

I don't want you to think your journey ends with this book. It doesn't, and it definitely shouldn't. This should be the beginning of your path in the financial world. The world of money is changing, and there are always new things to learn. Join online communities of young investors, find mentors who can guide you, read financial news, and everything else to make you more savvy in this industry. Also, you have to start using what you've learned right now if you haven't already. Open a savings account, download that budgeting app we talked about, research your first investment, and make a plan for your next paycheck. The sooner you get the ball rolling, the sooner you accomplish your dreams.

Why should you keep all of this knowledge to yourself? Share what you've learned with your friends. Explain compound interest to them; you might even be able to teach your parents a thing or two. When you picked up this book and read it until the last page, you made a decision about getting serious about your financial future. So, well done to you. This isn't all about money; it's about learning about you and setting yourself up for success. As the old

Chinese proverb goes, "The best time to plant a tree was twenty years ago; the second best time is now (Smith, 2015)." You're planting your financial tree earlier than most, so just imagine how tall it will grow.

GLOSSARY

Allowance: Money given on a regular basis (usually by your parents) that helps you practice budgeting and saving.

Budget: Your strategy for managing money and tracking what comes in (income) and what goes out (expenses).

Compound interest: One of the best savings tricks. When you earn interest, you're not only earning it from the money you deposited but also from previous interest.

Credit card: A card that allows you to borrow money to buy things. But don't forget to try to pay it in full!

Digital wallet: Apps like Venmo and Cash App let you spend money electronically, just like having a wallet on your phone.

Emergency fund: Money you save for unexpected stuff.

ESG investing: Investing in companies that care about the world we live in.

Financial ethics: Making money decisions that don't just benefit you but are also morally right.

Investment: Using your money to buy stocks or bonds that could be worth more later.

Passive income: Money you earn without actively working for it.

Philanthropy: Using your money, time, or skills to help others.

Savings account: A bank account that pays you interest simply for keeping your money there.

Side hustle: Extra work you do to make additional money.

Tax: Money we pay to the government to fund public services.

Wants vs. needs: The difference between things you must have (needs) and things you'd like to have (wants).

REFERENCES

Allen, N. (2024, October 9). *How to make money as a teen*. Investopedia. https://www.investopedia.com/how-to-make-money-as-a-teen-7550056

The basics about cryptocurrency. (n.d.). Oswego. https://www.oswego.edu/cts/basics-about-cryptocurrency

Beattie, A. (2024, September 24). *The history of money: From barter to banknotes*. Investopedia. https://www.investopedia.com/articles/07/roots_of_money.asp

Chen, J. (2024, July 19). *REIT: What it is and how to invest*. Investopedia. https://www.investopedia.com/terms/r/reit.asp

Cho, R. (2020, December 16). *How buying stuff drives climate change*. Columbia Climate School. https://news.climate.columbia.edu/2020/12/16/buying-stuff-drives-climate-change/

Ctanujit Classes. (n.d.). *200 solved problem on economics*. https://www.ctanujit.org/uploads/2/5/3/9/25393293/economics_solution_book.pdf

Daugherty, G. (2024, November 7). *Can teenagers invest in Roth IRAs?* Investopedia. https://www.investopedia.com/can-teenagers-invest-in-roth-iras-4770663

DeNicola, L. (2023, November 5). What is a credit utilization rate? *Experian*. https://www.experian.com/blogs/ask-experian/credit-education/score-basics/credit-utilization-rate/

EricT_CulinaryLore. (2012, September 23). *Origin of the expression "worth your salt."* CulinaryLore. https://culinarylore.com/food-history:worth-your-salt/

FDIC. (2024). *Understanding deposit insurance | FDIC*. Fdic.gov. https://www.fdic.gov/resources/deposit-insurance/understanding-deposit-insurance

First State Community Bank. (2023, August 15). Wealth-building facts & hacks every teen should know. https://www.fscb.com/blog/wealth-building-tips-for-teens

FSCS. (n.d.). *Deposit protection Q&As - banks & building societies*. https://www.fscs.org.uk/industry-resources/deposit-protection-banks/

Godfrey, N. (2015, May 10). Money and ethics: Let's show our kids how they fit together. *Forbes*. https://www.forbes.com/sites/nealegodfrey/2015/05/10/money-and-ethics-lets-show-our-kids-how-they-fit-together/

Haden, J. (2024, May 31). *Warren Buffett says 1 habit is guaranteed to be the best investment you'll ever make*. Inc. https://www.inc.com/jeff-haden/warren-buffett-says-1-habit-is-guaranteed-to-be-best-investment-youll-ever-make-and-its-tax-free.html

Hall, M. (2023, June 1). *How the banking sector impacts our economy.* Investopedia. https://www.investopedia.com/ask/answers/032315/what-banking-sector.asp

Hayes, A. (2024, May 31). *Dotcom bubble definition.* Investopedia. https://www.investopedia.com/terms/d/dotcom-bubble.asp

How to teach teenagers about money. (n.d.). Money Helper. https://www.moneyhelper.org.uk/en/family-and-care/talk-money/how-to-help-teenagers-manage-their-money

The Investopedia Team. (2024, June 15). *Cryptocurrency explained with pros and cons for investment.* Investopedia. https://www.investopedia.com/terms/c/cryptocurrency.asp

Irby, L. (2024, March 23). 7 tips for spending money wisely. *Experian.* https://www.experian.com/blogs/ask-experian/tips-for-spending-money-wisely/

IRS. (n.d.). *Here's who needs to file a tax return in 2024.* https://www.irs.gov/newsroom/heres-who-needs-to-file-a-tax-return-in-2024

Kagan, J. (2024, June 11). *What is the 4.* Investopedia. https://www.investopedia.com/terms/f/four-percent-rule.asp

Lambarena, M. (2021, January 21). *How to choose a teen checking account.* NerdWallet. https://www.nerdwallet.com/article/banking/how-to-choose-a-teen-checking-account

Lodge, M. (2024, June 30). *10 successful young entrepreneurs.* Investopedia. https://www.investopedia.com/10-successful-young-entrepreneurs-4773310

One Family. (n.d.). *Top 5 money management tips for teens.* https://www.onefamily.com/savings/money-management-tips-for-teens/

Ramsey Solutions. (2023, January 11). *5 fun ways to teach compound interest.* Ramsey. https://www.ramseysolutions.com/financial-literacy/teaching-compound-interest

Reader Contributors. (2021, December). *What is the best tool for teaching a teen to manage money? Parents weigh in.* The Dollar Stretcher. https://thedollarstretcher.com/family-finances/best-tool-for-teaching-teen-to-manage-money/

Sham, J. (2024, November 15). Roth IRA contribution and income limits 2024 and 2024. *NerdWallet.* https://www.nerdwallet.com/article/investing/roth-ira-contribution-limits

Smith, R. H. (2015, April 14). The best time to plant a tree was 20 years ago, no matter. *Psychology Today.* https://www.psychologytoday.com/gb/blog/joy-and-pain/201504/the-best-time-plant-tree-was-20-years-ago-no-matter

Startup Archive. (2024, July 22). *Palmer Luckey explains how he built the first oculus VR headset at 16 years old.* https://www.startuparchive.org/p/palmer-luckey-explains-how-he-built-the-first-oculus-vr-headset-at-16-years-old

Team Revolut. (2024, October 15). How to teach teenagers about money. *Revolut.*

https://www.revolut.com/blog/post/how-to-help-teenagers-manage-their-money/

Tidy, J. (2024, November 3). Hunt for Bitcoin's elusive creator Satoshi Nakamoto hits another dead end. *BBC News*. https://www.bbc.co.uk/news/articles/c079zp2vy31o

Wade, J. (2024, July 15). *What teens need to know about cryptocurrency*. Investopedia. https://www.investopedia.com/what-teens-need-to-know-about-cryptocurrency-7152233

Ward, M. (2017, May 25). Mark Zuckerberg returns to the Harvard dorm room where Facebook was born. *Make It*. https://www.cnbc.com/2017/05/25/mark-zuckerberg-returns-to-the-harvard-dorm-where-facebook-was-born.html

Warren, K. (2024, July 20). *Credit tips for teens*. Investopedia. https://www.investopedia.com/credit-tips-for-teens-7152864

What is the CDIC? (n.d.). TD. https://www.td.com/ca/en/personal-banking/products/bank-accounts/cdic

IMAGES

Bogdan, R. (2018). Person holding pink suede long waller. In *Pexels*. https://www.pexels.com/photo/person-holding-pink-suede-long-waller-910122/

Danilyuk, P. (2020). Shallow focus of two people handshaking. In *Pexels*. https://www.pexels.com/photo/shallow-focus-of-two-people-handshaking-5520322/

Guccione, J. (2019). 100 US dollar banknotes. In *Pexels*. https://www.pexels.com/photo/100-us-dollar-banknotes-3483098/

Jopwell. (2019). Woman in blue suit jacket. In *Pexels*. https://www.pexels.com/photo/woman-in-blue-suit-jacket-2422293/

Kabbompics. (2020). Person counting cash money. In *Pexels*. https://www.pexels.com/photo/person-counting-cash-money-4475523/

Kaboompics. (2020a). Close-up of woman counting dollar bills. In *Pexels*. https://www.pexels.com/photo/close-up-of-woman-counting-dollar-bills-5902919/

Kaboompics. (2020b). Crop anonymous person calculating profit on smartphone calculator near banknotes. In *Pexels*. https://www.pexels.com/photo/crop-anonymous-person-calculating-profit-on-smartphone-calculator-near-banknotes-4386321/

Lopez, J. (2024). Modern online shopping with mobile payment. In *Pexels*. https://www.pexels.com/photo/modern-online-shopping-with-mobile-payment-29502376/

Media, K. (2021). Woman in white and black crew neck t-shirt and blue denim jeans riding bicycle during. In *Pexels*. https://www.pexels.com/photo/woman-in-white-and-black-crew-neck-t-shirt-and-blue-denim-jeans-riding-bicycle-during-6868273/

Nappy. (2018). Man reading newspaper while sitting near table with smartphone and cup. In *Pexels*. https://www.pexels.com/photo/man-reading-newspaper-while-sitting-near-table-with-smartphone-and-cup-935979/

Pixabay. (2016a). Coins on brown wood. In *Pexels*. https://www.pexels.com/photo/coins-on-brown-wood-210600/

Pixabay. (2016b). Gray and black laptop computer. In *Pexels*. https://www.pexels.com/photo/gray-and-black-laptop-computer-265087/

Pixabay. (2016c). Hard cash on a briefcase. In *Pexels*. https://www.pexels.com/photo/hard-cash-on-a-briefcase-259027/

Pixabay. (2016d). Selective focus photo of stacked coins. In *Pexels*. https://www.pexels.com/photo/selective-focus-photo-of-stacked-coins-128867/

Pixabay. (2017a). 100 u.s. dollar banknotes. In *Pexels*. https://www.pexels.com/photo/100-u-s-dollar-banknotes-534229/

Pixabay. (2017b). Numbers on monitor. In *Pexels*. https://www.pexels.com/photo/numbers-on-monitor-534216/

rimthong, maitree. (2018). Person putting coin in a piggy bank. In *Pexels*. https://www.pexels.com/photo/person-putting-coin-in-a-piggy-bank-1602726/

Summer, L. (2020a). Crop anonymous person showing donation box. In *Pexels*. https://www.pexels.com/photo/crop-anonymous-person-showing-donation-box-6348119/

Summer, L. (2020b). Crop ethnic trader with smartphone and laptop on bench indoors. In *Pexels*. https://www.pexels.com/photo/crop-ethnic-trader-with-smartphone-and-laptop-on-bench-indoors-6347720/

Winstead, T. (2021). Close-Up shot of dollar bills. In *Pexels*. https://www.pexels.com/photo/close-up-shot-of-dollar-bills-7111611/

Printed in Dunstable, United Kingdom